Automation of Labor

Other Books of Related Interest

Opposing Viewpoints Series

Artificial Intelligence and the Technological Singularity
The Impact of the Tech Giants
Robotic Technology
Unemployment

At Issue Series

Are Unions Still Relevant?
The Right to a Living Wage
What Are the Jobs of the Future?
What Is the Future of the US Economy?

Current Controversies Series

Jobs in America
Privacy and Security in the Digital Age
The US Economy
The World Economy

> "Congress shall make no law … abridging the freedom of speech, or of the press."

First Amendment to the US Constitution

The basic foundation of our democracy is the First Amendment guarantee of freedom of expression. The Opposing Viewpoints series is dedicated to the concept of this basic freedom and the idea that it is more important to practice it than to enshrine it.

OPPOSING
VIEWPOINTS®
SERIES

Automation of Labor

Rachel Bozek, Book Editor

GREENHAVEN
PUBLISHING

Published in 2020 by Greenhaven Publishing, LLC
353 3rd Avenue, Suite 255, New York, NY 10010

Library of Congress Cataloging-in-Publication Data

Names: Bozek, Rachel, editor.
Title: Automation of labor / Rachel Bozek, book editor.
Description: First edition. | New York : Greenhaven Publishing, 2020. |
  Series: Opposing viewpoints | Includes bibliographical references and
  index. | Audience: Grades 9–12.
Identifiers: LCCN 2018060611| ISBN 9781534505063 (library bound) | ISBN
  9781534505070 (pbk.)
Subjects: LCSH: Labor supply—Effect of automation on—Juvenile literature. |
  Unemployment—Juvenile literature.
Classification: LCC HD6331 .A93185 2020 | DDC 331.25—dc23
LC record available at https://lccn.loc.gov/2018060611

Manufactured in the United States of America

Website: http://greenhavenpublishing.com

Contents

Chapter 3: Will the Automation of Labor Generate Any New Growth?

Chapter 4: Are We Headed Toward a Jobless Future?

The Importance of Opposing Viewpoints

Perhaps every generation experiences a period in time in which the populace seems especially polarized, starkly divided on the important issues of the day and gravitating toward the far ends of the political spectrum and away from a consensus-facilitating middle ground. The world that today's students are growing up in and that they will soon enter into as active and engaged citizens is deeply fragmented in just this way. Issues relating to terrorism, immigration, women's rights, minority rights, race relations, health care, taxation, wealth and poverty, the environment, policing, military intervention, the proper role of government—in some ways, perennial issues that are freshly and uniquely urgent and vital with each new generation—are currently roiling the world.

If we are to foster a knowledgeable, responsible, active, and engaged citizenry among today's youth, we must provide them with the intellectual, interpretive, and critical-thinking tools and experience necessary to make sense of the world around them and of the all-important debates and arguments that inform it. After all, the outcome of these debates will in large measure determine the future course, prospects, and outcomes of the world and its peoples, particularly its youth. If they are to become successful members of society and productive and informed citizens, students need to learn how to evaluate the strengths and weaknesses of someone else's arguments, how to sift fact from opinion and fallacy, and how to test the relative merits and validity of their own opinions against the known facts and the best possible available information. The landmark series Opposing Viewpoints has been providing students with just such critical-thinking skills and exposure to the debates surrounding society's most urgent contemporary issues for many years, and it continues to serve this essential role with undiminished commitment, care, and rigor.

The key to the series's success in achieving its goal of sharpening students' critical-thinking and analytic skills resides in its title—

Opposing Viewpoints. In every intriguing, compelling, and engaging volume of this series, readers are presented with the widest possible spectrum of distinct viewpoints, expert opinions, and informed argumentation and commentary, supplied by some of today's leading academics, thinkers, analysts, politicians, policy makers, economists, activists, change agents, and advocates. Every opinion and argument anthologized here is presented objectively and accorded respect. There is no editorializing in any introductory text or in the arrangement and order of the pieces. No piece is included as a "straw man," an easy ideological target for cheap point-scoring. As wide and inclusive a range of viewpoints as possible is offered, with no privileging of one particular political ideology or cultural perspective over another. It is left to each individual reader to evaluate the relative merits of each argument—as he or she sees it, and with the use of ever-growing critical-thinking skills—and grapple with his or her own assumptions, beliefs, and perspectives to determine how convincing or successful any given argument is and how the reader's own stance on the issue may be modified or altered in response to it.

This process is facilitated and supported by volume, chapter, and selection introductions that provide readers with the essential context they need to begin engaging with the spotlighted issues, with the debates surrounding them, and with their own perhaps shifting or nascent opinions on them. In addition, guided reading and discussion questions encourage readers to determine the authors' point of view and purpose, interrogate and analyze the various arguments and their rhetoric and structure, evaluate the arguments' strengths and weaknesses, test their claims against available facts and evidence, judge the validity of the reasoning, and bring into clearer, sharper focus the reader's own beliefs and conclusions and how they may differ from or align with those in the collection or those of their classmates.

Research has shown that reading comprehension skills improve dramatically when students are provided with compelling, intriguing, and relevant "discussable" texts. The subject matter of these collections could not be more compelling, intriguing, or urgently relevant to today's students and the world they are poised to inherit. The anthologized articles and the reading and discussion questions that are included with them also provide the basis for stimulating, lively, and passionate classroom debates. Students who are compelled to anticipate objections to their own argument and identify the flaws in those of an opponent read more carefully, think more critically, and steep themselves in relevant context, facts, and information more thoroughly. In short, using discussable text of the kind provided by every single volume in the Opposing Viewpoints series encourages close reading, facilitates reading comprehension, fosters research, strengthens critical thinking, and greatly enlivens and energizes classroom discussion and participation. The entire learning process is deepened, extended, and strengthened.

For all of these reasons, Opposing Viewpoints continues to be exactly the right resource at exactly the right time—when we most need to provide readers with the critical-thinking tools and skills that will not only serve them well in school but also in their careers and their daily lives as decision-making family members, community members, and citizens. This series encourages respectful engagement with and analysis of opposing viewpoints and fosters a resulting increase in the strength and rigor of one's own opinions and stances. As such, it helps make readers "future ready," and that readiness will pay rich dividends for the readers themselves, for the citizenry, for our society, and for the world at large.

Introduction

> *"Societies everywhere will have important choices to make in response to these challenges. Some may be tempted to try to halt or slow the adoption of automation. Even if this were possible ... it would mean foregoing the beneficial productivity effects the technology would bring."*
> —James Manyika and Michael Spence,
> *Harvard Business Review*

From changes in manufacturing to technological advances in software and other computer-run machines and tasks, automation is nothing if not unavoidable. The obvious—and reasonable—concern is that jobs, increasingly, will be replaced as automation continues, and we will fall deep into a state of technological unemployment, when large numbers of people lose their jobs to machines. The debate over whether this is truly the way things will go in the coming years is a lively one, ranging from conversations about a complete and utter loss of jobs being a sure thing to a celebration of the myriad benefits and added employment opportunities that will surely come out of this shift into a world of far higher productivity.

At the forefront of the technological unemployment concern is artificial intelligence (AI), which is becoming more and more sophisticated every year. Once just the stuff of science fiction, it's now used—or at least talked about—for work previously performed only by humans. AI is the clear next level of progression—the new horizon for where we, as a society, are headed.

However, the discussion between proponents of the wonders of technological advancements and believers in the potential for what some say could be unprecedented job loss is strong and long. The sides of this debate were clearly identified and explained by Stephen Hawking when he said, "The rise of powerful AI will either be the best or the worst thing ever to happen to humanity," at a speech in Cambridge in 2016. His concerns bridged the gap within this discussion, as he pointed to his already-established belief that there's little difference between what can be accomplished by a biological brain versus a computer. Expressing his anticipation of the positives, like eliminating poverty, to his worries about the ultimate negatives, like increased warfare and economic strife, Hawking urged experts and stakeholders at all levels of this movement to think ahead and utilize artificial intelligence only in ways that will result in positive changes for society. Several of the viewpoints in this book expand on his ideas and concerns from both sides.

Automation in manufacturing is quite different from automation in retail, and then yet again, playing to the beat of a completely different drummer is automation in service, creative industries, and education—namely personalized learning. And the idea that the jobs at risk of disappearing are exclusively blue collar in nature is quickly squashed as AI becomes a more prevalent element of the automation story.

Still, automation of labor is nothing new. It has been shaping and reshaping the workforce since the Industrial Revolution, when many people were forced to move from farm labor to factory work. Later, as the digital age began, there would be another shift from factory manufacturing to so-called white collar jobs. Is the latest workforce change cause for dread or is it an exciting new frontier?

The perspectives in *Opposing Viewpoints: Automation of Labor* explore the ideas of both sides of this discussion. As we learn more about productivity growth and employment growth—and relative pay increases—we are reminded that they do not happen in a linear or even predictable way. In chapters titled "Does the Automation of Labor Diminish Job Opportunities?," "Is Resistance to the Automation of Labor Just a Present-Day Version of the

Luddite Fallacy?," "Will the Automation of Labor Generate Any New Growth?," and "Are We Headed Toward a Jobless Future?," authors cover many of the issues and nuances surrounding the discussion of whether or not the automation of labor is ultimately a good idea.

OPPOSING
VIEWPOINTS®
SERIES

CHAPTER 1

Does the Automation of Labor Diminish Job Opportunities?

Chapter Preface

A s the prevalence of automation has increased over recent decades, so has the expectation that this is the way most industries are headed. And that means fewer jobs for the population at large, right? That is true for many cases. But not all. The question of whether the phenomenon of automation leads to a decrease in job opportunities is an often-debated topic, with some experts arguing that the rise of automation will make humans, essentially, obsolete in many industries.

According to the US Bureau of Labor and Statistics (BLS), 62.6 million jobs were lost in 2017. However, it should be noted that 64.7 jobs were *created*, resulting in a net increase of more than 2 million jobs.

Many people across industries that implement automation believe that increased automation will simply make way for new and different opportunities for those who lose their jobs due to the technological advances in certain industries. The numbers above support this.

In many cases, however, cause for concern stems from the following: as automation of certain tasks increases, a need for people to execute those tasks becomes less necessary. It should be noted, says the other side, that while certain specific tasks are automated, the fact remains that people *will* continue to be needed in completing the "whole job."

The automation of labor makes finding entry-level employment more challenging for recent graduates and individuals changing careers, especially in certain fields—manufacturing in particular. Still, it leads to increased opportunity elsewhere, such as retail and service.

Viewpoints in the following chapter argue that the automation of labor does not pose a threat to employment opportunities and that automation has some potential benefits, such as eliminating the drudgery of work. Others encourage careful consideration of the implications of such progress and preparation of "good jobs" so as to maintain the workforce in numbers that makes sense.

| "As long as there are unmet needs in society, there will be work to be done."

Labor Opportunities Are Not Threatened by Automation

Mark Paul

In the following excerpted viewpoint, Mark Paul argues that the automation of labor does not pose a threat to employment opportunities. While he acknowledges the short-term cost of such a transition, he suggests policy changes that could serve as solutions to rectify the disconnect between productivity levels that are not particularly high (along with slow capital investment) now compared to what it would look like during a time when automation was potentially posing a threat. These include a recommitment on the part of the United States to full employment, a revision of intellectual property law, a focus on technological developments and innovations that work for the labor force, implementing work-sharing practices, and making education and training more universally accessible. Paul is a fellow at the Roosevelt Institute, which strives to answer the question of what a better society looks like.

As you read, consider the following questions:

1. Would mass unemployment be inevitable if we were in fact on the cusp of immediate technological change?
2. What should happen to the lengths of patents and copyright protections in order to rectify the broken link between productivity growth and appropriate wages?
3. How should work sharing be implemented as a solution?

The narrative that large-scale automation will imminently lead to mass unemployment and economic insecurity has become prevalent in the media. As the story goes, we are on the cusp of a major technological change that will drastically alter the nature of work, leave masses unemployed, and exacerbate already high levels of economic inequality.

In this paper, we argue that this narrative detracts from the bigger underlying problems with the rules of our economy and the distributional consequences of increased automation under current institutional arrangements.

First, we find that there is little evidence to suggest that the U.S. economy is approaching massive technological change: productivity levels are remarkably low and capital investment is significantly slower than would be expected under impending technological upheaval. Second, historical evidence suggests that even if we were on the verge of rapid technological change, mass unemployment would not be inevitable. In the past, the long-term effects of technological advancement on employment have been positive. Technology has allowed workers to do their jobs better and faster, which in turn, increased output and raised living standards.

As with any major structural shift in the economy, technological change has the potential to create job loss in the short term but does not necessarily lead to net job destruction in the long term. The amount of work available is not a fixed quantity, and technology can complement labor, instead of substitute for it, making workers more productive rather than simply replacing them. The job gains from technology often outpace the job losses over time and allow workers to focus on better, high-productivity jobs.

However, we should not trivialize the costs of this kind of economic transition for workers in the short term, nor can we ignore the structural disadvantages in today's economy that define economic outcomes. Workers are right to be concerned about the negative effects of technological change because the historical link between labor productivity and wages, which grew side-by-side for most of the 20th century, is broken. In the past, productivity growth from technological innovation led to shared prosperity for workers, including higher wages and better living standards. When that link broke, it changed how the economic pie was divided.

In order to fix this broken link, we propose a few policy changes that would ensure that economic growth from technological change benefits everyone:

- Full employment: The U.S. government should recommit to pursuing full employment. Implementing full employment would create a significantly tighter labor market, which would both encourage technological advance and nullify the potential negative effects of technology on workers.
- Revised intellectual property law: Intellectual property law is a primary reason why technological advances currently exacerbate inequality. While a first step would be reducing the lengths of patents and copyright protections, more substantial measures should also be pursued.
- Public guidance in technological development: Government has a sizeable role in leading the direction of innovation through funding research and establishing research agencies. The government should focus on tech innovations that complement workers.
- Work sharing: The U.S. should adopt work sharing in two ways. First, in reducing the overall hours typically worked by individuals; and second, by temporarily reducing working hours during economic downturns, rather than laying off workers.

- Free higher education and vocational training: Education and training are vital components in advancing society and maintaining a productive workforce. More accessible options should be made available to the public.

While these are not a comprehensive list of potential policy changes, they provide a starting point for moving toward an economy where all workers share the gains from technological advancement.

[…]

Many are concerned with the idea that automation will displace workers—and they are partially right, though the story is not so simple. There have been, and will continue to be, innovations that replace workers throughout the economy. But those workers are only permanently displaced if we think there is a fixed amount of work to be done in the economy. This idea, which gives rise to the notion that an increase in the amount each worker can produce actually reduces the total number of jobs an economy can support, is known as the "lump-of-labor fallacy."

Think about the personal secretary. The advent of the computer, combined with advances in software, have led to the decline of this profession. This undoubtedly displaced hundreds of thousands of workers (Jacobs 2015). Do these workers permanently leave the labor market? Are those jobs gone forever, never to be replaced by other jobs? If we think there is only a fixed amount of work to be done in the economy, we would rightly want to bash these machines. After all, they will take all the work!

But that is not how the real economy functions. First, our economy is a dynamic one. Every month, new jobs are created as other jobs are destroyed. When we read the headline numbers from the U.S. Bureau of Labor and Statistics (BLS) on job creation every month, what we are seeing is the difference between jobs created and jobs destroyed. Luckily, the government tracks these numbers in the BLS Job Openings and Labor Turnover Survey (JOLTS). In 2017, the economy destroyed 62.6 million jobs—but it also created 64.7 million, meaning that the economy added 2.2 million net jobs (BLS 2018b). The economy will continue to destroy specific jobs, but that is not necessarily a bad thing for the overall economy. To be sure, the personal consequences from losing a job can be catastrophic. For this reason, policymakers should improve social insurance programs, support policies to aid in rapidly transitioning workers to new jobs, and push for permanent full employment through direct government hiring.

On average, the economy destroys low-productivity jobs and replaces them with higher-productivity jobs—opening the door for higher wages and rising living standards.

Second, we do not know what the jobs of the future are. A generation ago, people would not have predicted that information technology (IT) jobs would be where they are today. It is clear from the media reports that the fear of destroying jobs sells. What is missed by this half-truth is the fact that technological developments also generate new jobs. As the recent Deloitte report argues, technology creates far more jobs than it destroys (Stewart et al. 2018).

Third, the fallacy misdirects public policies. Arguments are frequently made that we need to bring back our old jobs or rejuvenate declining industries like coal. Given the destruction of communities in the wake of increased trade and an economy transitioning away from coal and general manufacturing, such arguments are understandable. But policies directed to look backward instead of forward are misguided. While this does little to combat the economic despair caused by losing these jobs, the answer is in building public policies for the future. The fatalism perpetuated by the lump-of-labor fallacy, inciting fear that the economy cannot create new and better jobs, leads to a decline in public pressure on policymakers to help create an economy with full employment and rising wages. Policymakers must recognize and adapt to the fact that the economy is dynamic, but also that getting the policies right is essential to the creation of new and better jobs. After all, the level of unemployment and wages in our modern economy is largely dictated by policy choices.

In sum, as long as there are unmet needs in society, there will be work to be done.

| *"While automation may replace some jobs, the technology rarely acts as a substitute for people."*

It's Time to Stop the "End of Work" Hysteria

Tony Dundon and Debra Howcroft

In the following viewpoint, Tony Dundon and Debra Howcroft argue that ideas like a semi-autonomous Driver Pilot system could potentially free up a substantial amount of time currently spent on what they refer to as the "drudgery of work." They look to the digital future as a freeing element of where work is headed, not as a road to nowhere for the workforce. Ultimately, they say, politics and economics will remain the driving forces in the development and implementation of technology. From where they sit, "capitalist relations and geopolitical systems of governance" will simply not allow for an "end of work" phenomenon. Dundon is a professor of HRM and employment relations and Howcroft is a professor of technology and organization, both at the University of Manchester.

"Automation, Robots and the 'End of Work' Myth," by Tony Dundon and Debra Howcroft, The Conversation, January 16, 2018. https://theconversation.com/automation-robots-and -the-end-of-work-myth-89619. Licensed under CC BY-ND 4.0 International.

As you read, consider the following questions:

1. Who made the argument that technology would help free workers from harsh labor and lead to a "reduction to working time"?
2. What concept builds on existing inequalities in a society, rather than wiping them away?
3. What are corporations looking to maximize, according to the article?

C an you imagine travelling to work in a robotic "Jonnycab" like the one predicted in the cult Arnold Schwarzenegger movie *Total Recall*? The image from 1990 is based on science fiction, but Mercedes Benz does have a semi-autonomous Driver Pilot system that it aims to install in the next five years and Uber is also waging on a self-driving future. Its partnership with Volvo has been seen as a boost to its ambitions to replace a fleet of self-employed drivers with autonomous vehicles.

Jonnycab might belong to futurology but if MIT academics Erik Brynjolfson and Andrew McAfee are right, we may all be rejoicing at the prospect of extended leisure time, as robotic technologies free us from the drudgery of work. Except for the fact that big business will be keeping its eye on the bottom line and will often be opting for fast and cheap alternatives.

No Work, More Play?

These are not new concepts. Karl Marx argued technology would help free workers from harsh labour and lead to a "reduction to working time." In the 1930s Bertrand Russell wrote of the benefits of "a little more idleness" and the economist John Maynard Keynes predicted that automation could enable a shorter working week of less than 15 hours.

Claims that robotics will wipe out millions of jobs, from car manufacturing to banking are all too common. But some see a change to how we work running alongside these job losses.

Empowering or Enslaving?

Instead, some envision that digital platforms will empower people to become their own boss with the freedom to choose when and where to work and how much they will earn. And people will be encouraged to earn a living by "mixing it up"—becoming a driver one day (using the Uber or Deliveroo app) and then switching to digital "microtasks" (a small unit of work such as tagging images or translating text that takes place on a virtual assembly line) on one of the burgeoning platforms that make up the gig economy.

A future where work is replaced by leisure time has widespread appeal. But the reality is many people now work longer hours with growing job insecurity, fragmented income and labour market precariousness. If anything, technology has not liberated people from the drudgery of work as Marx, Russell and Keynes once anticipated, but has created new constraints, invading people's social and leisure time through the digitalisation of life.

While technology may displace older job skills, new work demands emerge. Most corporations seek to protect their vested interests (maximising profit) while keeping shareholders sweet, which often means searching for cheaper labour rather than investing in expensive capital infrastructures.

The ability to use technology to automate does not necessarily lead to implementation. Of the US companies that could benefit from robots, only 10% have opted to do so. For low-skilled and low-paid sectors—including care homes, restaurants, bars and some factories—it will continue to be less costly to employ people.

Consider the last time you had your car washed. The chances are it was not an automated drive-through, but a hand-wash carried out by immigrant labour at lower cost than the automated alternative. In short, while labour remains cheap, employers tend to cash in rather than benefit from the full potential of technologies.

Many employers have little intention of innovating through technology. Consumerism and an almost blind faith in free market principles mean technology is leveraged to extract ever greater profit, rather than provide some of the idleness and leisure time Bertrand Russell felt would benefit society.

No Substitute for People

Technology and how it is developed and adopted is not a neutral force but is shaped by politics and economics. While automation may replace some jobs, the technology rarely acts as a substitute for people. Instead, jobs become codified and reduced to a narrow range of de-skilled tasks. Technology is deeply connected to relations of power and tends not to wipe away inequalities in a society, but builds on existing inequalities.

The proliferation of digital technologies can be associated with the growth of insecure, intensive and poor quality work as seen in Amazon warehouses and Foxconn (a major manufacturer of Apple products) who use technology to monitor performance and dehumanise the workplace. The net effect is a polarised labour market of low-skill and low-income workers sitting alongside an elite who enjoy more secure jobs (at least for now).

The future of work seems more likely to revolve around cost-containment strategies which limit investment in infrastructure and efficient technologies, opting instead for cheap sweated labour. It is more likely that managers will forego efficiency-generating gains from digital technologies because of a fear of losing control. Remember the promise of homeworking in the electronic cottage?

In order to realise Keynes' vision of a shorter working week, managers would have to share control and provide an employment regime supporting genuine self-determination. Unfortunately, modern capitalist relations and geopolitical systems of governance are intolerant of such egalitarianism. For these reasons, it's time to draw a close to the "end of work" hysteria. It is sham.

"While many low-skill jobs are being eliminated, positions demanding higher skills are being created."

Changes in the Workforce Are a Direct Result of Automation

Steve Bates

In the following viewpoint, Steve Bates argues that shifting job descriptions and responsibilities of professionals will be strongly influenced by advances in technology as they pertain to automation. He points to the challenge of employers needing to be able to identify just how automation fits into their businesses and likely having trouble doing so. Certain types of jobs, like travel agent, meter reader, flight attendant, and lumberjack, are at far greater risk of being eliminated or drastically reduced as a result of automation than jobs like doctors, nurses, entertainers, and other positions that rely on human interaction and creativity. It will be a challenge for employers to support their team members who might move up into higher ranks if they themselves don't understand what those new jobs will entail. Bates is a former writer and editor for the Society for Human Resource Management.

As you read, consider the following questions:

1. What kinds of jobs are diminishing?
2. What kinds of jobs will there always be a need for?
3. What kinds of institutions can employers work with to help better prepare future employees?

An unstoppable wave of automation is transforming the workplace. While many low-skill jobs are being eliminated, positions demanding higher skills are being created. Most jobs in existence today will add and lose specific functions in the future as robots and other forms of technology take on routine tasks and free humans to focus more on creative and analytic efforts, according to experts.

It will be a messy transition. It will be particularly painful for workers who lose their jobs and for employers that fail to recognize where automation fits into their operations.

Labor market experts disagree about how many American jobs will be lost to automation. A 2013 report by Oxford University researchers concluded that about 47 percent of total U.S. employment is at risk because of automation. A 2015 report by McKinsey & Co. forecast that automation could eliminate as much as 45 percent of work activities currently performed in the U.S.

Forrester Research predicts that robots—all forms of automation, machine learning and intelligent machines—will replace 16 percent of American jobs but will create the equivalent of 9 percent of those jobs by 2025. That would represent a net loss of 7 percent of jobs.

"This transition has, in fact, been going on for decades," said a 2016 Forrester report, The Future Of White-Collar Work: Sharing Your Cubicle With Robots. For example, software "bots" are already scheduling humans' meetings online, handling travel request forms and processing employment contracts. Intelligent devices are helping manage warehouses and parking garages to boost efficiency. IBM's supercomputer Watson, which defeated humans on the quiz show "Jeopardy," is working with doctors to improve diagnoses of patients' diseases.

Among the traditional jobs most endangered by automation are travel agent, meter reader, flight attendant, lumberjack, librarian and newspaper reporter.

The loss of jobs is a particularly hot issue in the 2016 elections. Labor market experts point to automation and globalization as the primary reasons for jobs being eliminated or shifted overseas. They note that transformations such as these have happened frequently during history.

"For centuries, humans have feared machines," said Harry J. Holzer, a professor of public policy at Georgetown University in Washington, D.C. "Their worst fears have never turned out to be true." Experts say that while there are always winners and losers in these transitions, the big-picture view is that technology will boost productivity and fuel the economy.

Shifting Roles

Occupations focusing on human interaction, such as doctor, nurse and massage therapist, will be among those most immune to being replaced by robots. Flesh-and-blood artists, designers, athletes and entertainers also will retain a place in society. New jobs attributable to the rise of automation will include software developers and managers who can integrate automation technology into existing business models. People will work directly with robots to help them learn new functions or handle their tasks better, though the robots might not look like humans and the human-robot communication will occur mostly via keyboard.

The shifting of job tasks from humans to robots will require a massive change in job descriptions, not to mention in talent acquisition strategies. According to Forrester, automation will change every job category by at least 25 percent as soon as 2019. "Few firms are prepared for their [cognitive tipping points], which

STEPHEN HAWKING'S PREDICTION

In a column in The Guardian, the world-famous physicist wrote that "the automation of factories has already decimated jobs in traditional manufacturing, and the rise of artificial intelligence is likely to extend this job destruction deep into the middle classes, with only the most caring, creative or supervisory roles remaining."

He adds his voice to a growing chorus of experts concerned about the effects that technology will have on workforce in the coming years and decades. The fear is that while artificial intelligence will bring radical increases in efficiency in industry, for ordinary people this will translate into unemployment and uncertainty, as their human jobs are replaced by machines.

Automation "in turn will accelerate the already widening economic inequality around the world," Hawking wrote. "The internet and the platforms that it makes possible allow very small groups of individuals to make enormous profits while employing very few people. This is inevitable, it is progress, but it is also socially destructive."

He frames this economic anxiety as a reason for the rise in right-wing, populist politics in the West: "We are living in a world of widening, not diminishing, financial inequality, in which many people can see not just their standard of living, but their ability to earn a living at all, disappearing. It is no wonder then that they are searching for a new deal, which Trump and Brexit might have appeared to represent."

Combined with other issues—overpopulation, climate change, disease—we are, Hawking warns ominously, at "the most dangerous moment in the development of humanity." Humanity must come together if we are to overcome these challenges, he says.

Stephen Hawking has previously expressed concerns about artificial intelligence for a different reason—that it might overtake and replace humans. "The development of artificial intelligence could spell the end of the human race," he said in late 2014. "It would take off on its own, and redesign itself at an ever increasing rate. Humans, who are limited by slow biological evolution, couldn't compete, and would be superseded."

"Stephen Hawking: This will be the impact of automation and AI on jobs," by Rob Price, World Economic Forum, December 6, 2016.

will lead to a restructuring of work nearly as profound as the transition from the agricultural age to the industrial age," said its 2016 report.

The Training Challenge

Training future employees—and retraining current ones—will be an immense challenge in the face of the transformation. Experts say that workers will need skills related to a specific job function as well as broader competencies.

"Thriving in today's fast-changing world requires breadth of skills rooted in academic competencies such as literacy, numeracy and science but also including things such as teamwork, critical thinking, communication, persistence and creativity," according to the 2016 report Skills for a Changing World from the Brookings Institution, a Washington, D.C., think tank.

"Back in the 1970s, you took part of yourself to work. Now you take the whole person to work," said Anthony P. Carnevale, Ph.D., director of the Georgetown University Center on Education and the Workforce. "There's a much broader range of human competencies necessary."

For decades, employers have hired young people and trained them to do a particular job. Today, however, employers are expecting job applicants to be better prepared for jobs with highly technical requirements.

"Students can't learn everything once they get to the job," said Mary V.L. Wright, senior director of national career education advocacy group Jobs for the Future.

Educational systems can't turn on a dime, but "employers can help colleges figure out 'What are the competencies we require for this position' and 'Here's how we want you to teach them,'" said Angela Hanks, associate director of workforce development policy at the Center for American Progress, a progressive public-policy advocacy organization.

"We need to contextualize skills to the needs of today's economy," said Maria Flynn, senior vice president of Jobs for the

Future. She said that, to minimize disruption, employers "can embed learning in an individual's job to prepare them for the next job."

Retraining displaced workers is particularly difficult. Some of them lack the fundamental skills that are prerequisites to learning today's sophisticated job functions. Training programs are fragmented, and many are not matched closely to the emerging needs of employers.

"How do you prepare people for jobs that are not really there yet?" Hanks asked.

While some local and regional job training partnerships involving employers have shown great promise—and apprenticeships are drawing increasing interest from employers—the best programs are not large and widespread enough to make a big dent in the ranks of the unemployed.

Experts say it's difficult to predict exactly how the technology revolution will play out. But they offer some solace to employers: Don't expect to see robots asking for raises or organizing their own labor unions anytime soon.

| "Are we living in an era so different
than past periods of change?"

Experts Are Divided on the Future Job Market

David Trilling

In the following viewpoint, David Trilling argues that the future workforce will need to develop more creative skills and will need more education, along the lines of the changes the United States saw in the late nineteenth century. However, experts are divided on whether job creation will outpace or fall behind the rate at which jobs are eliminated. Some, like Stephen Hawking, have expressed the sentiment that artificial intelligence will leave "only the most caring, creative or supervisory roles remaining" and "accelerate the already widening economic inequality around the world," while others, like Boston University economist James Bessen, argue that the widespread implementation of automated teller machines (ATMs) most certainly did not lead to a loss of total tellers as it resulted in a clear increase in the number of banks operating. Trilling is the managing editor of Eurasianet and was a staff writer for Journalist's Resource from 2016 to 2018.

As you read, consider the following questions:

1. What US industry eliminated about three-quarters of its workforce between 1962 and 2005, as a result of increased automation?
2. Who agrees that a retraining of the workforce will be required as technology changes and automation becomes more prevalent?
3. What types of deals do some US politicians say are job killers?

Over the next 15 years, 2 to 3 million Americans who drive for a living—truckers, bus drivers and cabbies—will be replaced by self-driving vehicles, according to a December 2016 White House report on the ascent of artificial intelligence (AI). An estimate by the University of Oxford and Citi, a bank, predicts that 77 percent of Chinese jobs are at risk of automation over roughly the same period.

Millions of people around the world would lose their jobs under these scenarios, potentially sparking mass social unrest and upheaval.

Yet mechanization has always been a feature of modern economies. For example, while American steel output remained roughly even between 1962 and 2005, the industry shed about 75 percent of its workforce, or 400,000 employees, according to a 2015 paper in the *American Economic Review*. Since 1990, the United States has lost 30 percent (5.5 million) of its manufacturing jobs while manufacturing output has grown 148 percent, according to data from the Federal Reserve Bank of St. Louis.

Machines are besting humans in more and more tasks; thanks to technology, fewer Americans make more stuff in less time. But today economists debate not whether machines are changing the workplace and making us more efficient—they certainly are—but whether the result is a net loss of jobs. The figures above may look dire. But since 1990, the total non-farm workforce has grown 33 percent, more than accounting for the manufacturing jobs lost.

As we look ahead to a world populated by smart machines that can learn ever more complex tasks, economists agree that retraining people will be required. And—as is the case with global free trade—any big economic shift creates both winners and losers. What they don't agree on is the degree to which machines will replace people.

Occupations and Tasks: Quantifying Jobs Lost

Robots are easier to manage than people, Hardee's CEO Andrew Puzder (Donald Trump's original pick for labor secretary) said in 2016: "They're always polite, they always upsell, they never take a vacation, they never show up late, there's never a slip-and-fall, or an age, sex, or race discrimination case."

According to the 2016 White House report, between 9 and 47 percent of American jobs could be made irrelevant by machines in the next two decades; most of those positions—like jobs at Hardee's—demand little training.

The 47 percent figure comes from a widely cited 2013 paper by Carl Benedikt Frey and Michael Osborne, both of the University of Oxford. Frey and Osborne ranked 702 jobs based on the "probability of computerization." Telemarketers, title examiners and hand sewers have a 99 percent chance of being replaced by machines, according to their methodology. Doctors and therapists are the least likely to be supplanted. In the middle, with a 50 percent chance of automatization, are loading machine operators in underground mines, court reporters, and construction workers overseeing installation, maintenance and repair.

In a 2016 paper, the Organization for Economic Cooperation and Development (OECD)—a policy think tank run by 35 rich countries—took a different approach that looks at all the tasks that workers do; taking "account of the heterogeneity of workplace tasks within occupations already strongly reduces the predicted share of jobs that are at a high risk of automation." The paper found only 9 percent of jobs face high risk of automatization in the U.S. Across all 35 OECD member states, they found a range of 6 to 12 percent facing this high risk of automatization.

Job Gains

Are we living in an era so different than past periods of change? Industrialization gutted the skilled artisan class of the 19th century by automating processes like textile and candle making. The conversion generated so many new jobs that rural people crowded into cities to take factory positions. Over the 20th century, the ratio of farm jobs fell from 40 percent to 2 percent, yet farm productivity swelled. The technical revolution in the late 20th century moved workers from factories to new service-industry jobs.

Frey and Osborne argue that this time is different. New advances in artificial intelligence and mobile robotics mean machines are increasingly able to learn and perform non-routine tasks, such as driving a truck. Job losses will outpace the so-called capitalization effect, whereby new technologies that save time actually create jobs and speed up development, they say. Without the capitalization effect, unemployment rates will reach never-before-seen levels. The only jobs that remain will require workers to address challenges that cannot be addressed by algorithms.

Yet many prominent economists argue that this new age will not be so different than previous technological breakthroughs, that the gains will counter the losses.

Take ATMs, for example. Have they killed jobs? No, the number of bank jobs in the U.S. has increased at a healthy clip since ATMs were introduced, Boston University economist James Bessen showed in 2016: "Why didn't employment fall? Because the ATM allowed banks to operate branch offices at lower cost; this prompted them to open many more branches ... offsetting the erstwhile loss in teller jobs."

In a 2016 working paper for the National Bureau of Economic Research, Daron Acemoglu and Pascual Restrepo—economists at

MIT—describe two effects of automation. The technology increases productivity (think about that growth in steel output with fewer workers). This, in turn, creates a greater demand for workers to perform the more complex tasks that computers cannot handle. But that, Acemoglu and Restrepo say, is countered by a displacement effect—the people who are replaced by machines may not have suitable training to take on these more complicated jobs. As the workforce becomes better trained, wages rise. The authors conclude that "inequality increases during transitions, but the self-correcting forces in our model also limit the increase in inequality over the long-run."

Unlike Frey and Osborne, Acemoglu and Restrepo believe the pace of job creation will keep ahead of the rate of destruction.

At MIT, David Autor agrees. In a 2015 paper for the *Journal of Economic Perspectives*, Autor argues that "machines both substitute for and complement" workers. Automation "raises output in ways that lead to higher demand" for workers, "raising the value of the tasks that workers uniquely supply."

Journalists and newsrooms in the U.S. and Europe are the subject of a 2017 case study by Carl-Gustav Linden of the University of Helsinki, in Finland. Though algorithms are able to perform some of the most routine journalistic tasks, such as writing brief statements on earnings reports and weather forecasts, journalists are not disappearing. Rather, Linden finds "resilience in creative and artisanal jobs."

Education

Stephen Hawking, the eminent Cambridge physicist, warned in a 2016 op-ed for *The Guardian* that artificial intelligence will leave "only the most caring, creative or supervisory roles remaining" and "accelerate the already widening economic inequality around the world."

While such dire predictions are common in the mainstream press, economists urge caution.

"Journalists and even expert commentators tend to overstate the extent of machine substitution for human labor and ignore the strong complementarities between automation and labor that increase productivity, raise earnings, and augment demand for labor," wrote Autor in his 2015 paper.

This must be addressed, the White House stressed in its 2016 review, with investment in education, in retraining for older workers, and by strengthening the unemployment insurance system during periods of change.

Autor is sanguine about the government's ability to prepare workers for the high-tech jobs of tomorrow. "The ability of the U.S. education and job training system (both public and private) to produce the kinds of workers who will thrive in these middle-skill jobs of the future can be called into question," he wrote. "In this and other ways, the issue is not that middle-class workers are doomed by automation and technology, but instead that human capital investment must be at the heart of any long-term strategy."

Economists are basically unanimous: the jobs of the future will require more education and creative skills. (The last time the U.S. faced such a challenge, in the late 19th century, it invested heavily in high schools for all children.)

Even so, computers appear to be usurping knowledge jobs, too. IBM claims it has designed a computer that is better than a human doctor at diagnosing cancer; in Japan, an insurance company is replacing its underwriters with computers.

Globalization, Free Trade and Robots

Some American politicians often point at free trade deals, specifically with China and Mexico, as job-killing and bad for American workers. But a growing body of research points to machines as the real culprits. For example, a 2015 study published by Ball State University found that between 2000 and 2010, 88 percent of lost manufacturing jobs were taken by robots, while trade was responsible for 13.4 percent of lost jobs.

Machines cost about the same to operate no matter where they are located. If it costs the same to keep a factory in China or Ohio, a firm would probably prefer Ohio. Whether the firm is Chinese or American, in theory there is the rule of law in America to protect its investment. So for journalists, a question is not where these automated workshops of the future will be located. It is where the robots toiling in them will be made.

> *"The existence of high unemployment while jobs remain unfilled raises serious questions about the need for structural changes to ensure a better match of talent to the changing needs of the economy."*

We Should Prepare for Good Jobs, Not Just Any Jobs

Jessica Davis Pluess

In the following excerpted viewpoint, Jessica Davis Pluess argues that an investment in technology and automation must include consideration of the impacts these advances will have on the current and future labor force. This will ensure the best chances for remaining competitive in growth, productivity, and innovation. She notes that geographic areas of high unemployment, such as Asia and the Pacific, still face major challenges when it comes to finding appropriately qualified candidates. The challenge is not in creating and recruiting for "any" job, but rather in doing so for "good jobs." Davis Pluess is the challenge director, Switzerland, at Business Fights Poverty.

"Good Jobs in the Age of Automation," by Jessica Davis Pluess, Business for Social Responsibility (BSR), June 2015. Reprinted by permission.

As you read, consider the following questions:

1. Name three of the skills that the IFTF has identified as being essential for the future workforce.
2. When it's linked to higher wages and skill-building opportunities, what are a few of the areas where employers can expect to see increases?
3. Does the author support the idea of employers viewing human capital as a cost or as an investment?

E nabling more people to benefit from this era of technological change is in the best interest of business. Ensuring automation provides broad-based benefits to society—including the creation and preservation of good jobs—is essential to creating a strong talent pipeline that can foster innovation and capture the productivity gains presented by automation. Moreover, good jobs are a fundamental part of prosperous and resilient communities and vibrant economies, which are conditions for business success.

Continuing to invest in technology and automation without considering the impacts on the current and future labor force could lead to a host of operational and reputational risks as well as missed opportunities for business growth, productivity, and innovation. This section provides some perspectives on why it is important for companies to prepare and respond to this era of technology change in a way that creates broad-based benefits for society.

Accessing Talent and Innovation

As noted earlier, major automation trends will likely require new or enhanced skills among current and future workers. The Institute for the Future (IFTF) has identified 10 skills that are essential for the future workforce. It includes sense-making and social intelligence skills, which it believes will be in high demand as smart machines take over rote, routine manufacturing and services jobs. Workers that can harvest critical insights to inform decision-making and assess the emotions of those around them and adapt their words, tone, and gestures accordingly will also be in high demand. IFTF also identified quantitative reasoning skills and design mindset as increasingly attractive.[1]

Finding people with the right skills to fill many of the jobs created by technology could present human capital challenges for companies, particularly for certain industries that are already facing talent pipeline issues. PwC's latest Manufacturing Barometer survey found that difficulty finding/hiring skilled workers with robotics experience was the second greatest barrier to acquiring more robotics systems after cost.[2] The McKinsey Global Institute projects that the United States alone faces a shortage of 140,000 to 190,000 people with analytical expertise and 1.5 million managers and analysts with the skills to understand and make decisions based on the analysis of Big Data.[3]

While Asia and the Pacific accounts for almost half of global unemployment, 45 percent of employers in the region face difficulty in finding suitable talent in their markets, according to the Asian Development Bank.[4]

Chinese policymakers have set a target of 9 percent annual growth in the production of more sophisticated goods under its strategy of *tenglong huanniao*, which is intended to move away from low-cost manufacturing.[5] However, there are difficulties in recruiting enough skilled technicians to fill these jobs. The Chinese machinery sector alone projected a gap of 600,000 computer-automated machine tool operators in 2014, according to Reuters.[6]

In an interview with BSR, Liang Xiaohui of the China National Textile and Apparel Council noted that investments in building skills are an important part of China's strategy. "We have to evolve to a higher stage of the supply chain to compete," he argued. "Getting there will take two critical elements: The first one is to be innovative, for instance, upgrading technologies in manufacturing, and the second is building a workforce of people that can effectively work with and work for innovations. To support our efforts to upgrade our industry, we have to build up our human resources potential and give people, especially existing textile workers, more opportunities to learn expertise and skills."

The existence of high unemployment while jobs remain unfilled raises serious questions about the need for structural changes to ensure a better match of talent to the changing needs of the economy. Most academic experts believe that our current educational system is not adequately prepared to meet these needs. According to the European Commission, some 47 percent of European workers have insufficient digital skills and 23 percent have none at all.[7] In California, computing-related jobs outnumber annual Computer Science graduates by 16 to 1.[8]

As a source of innovation and productivity, companies that don't invest in building the right skills for current and future workforces could find it difficult to stay competitive.

Maintaining Positive Community Relations and Social License to Operate

The anticipated elimination of jobs could lead to "stranded human assets," workers who are displaced by changes to existing production models. Rising unemployment and a smaller share of workers capturing a larger share of the pie could affect social cohesion and pose reputational and operational risks for companies in the communities where they operate.

The World Bank has documented numerous cases where unemployment and/or downsizing of operations in communities (not necessarily as a result of automation) led to mistrust and disengagement in community life, all of which have implications for company relations with communities and social and economic progress.[9] While not directly the result of automation, any downward pressure on wages or cost-saving labor cuts can threaten community trust and civic engagement and challenge companies' social license to operate.

Cities like Youngstown, Ohio and Detroit, Michigan show how once bustling communities and vibrant local economies can suffer both economic disruption and social and cultural breakdown from a broad- scale decline in manufacturing employment. *The Atlantic* recently reported how Youngstown went from one of the highest median income and homeownership rates in the United States, during the height of steel manufacturing, to chronic economic depression after jobs moved to new manufacturing locations. Within five years, the city lost 50,000 jobs and $1.3 billion in manufacturing wages and saw depression, spousal abuse, and suicide become more prevalent.[10] While this wasn't driven by automation, if offshoring is "a way station on the road to automation," as some experts have argued,[11] it is not unreasonable to anticipate that some current manufacturing centers around the world could see similar fates.

This is important for companies who are considering eliminating jobs because they could see a rapid erosion of the goodwill established with communities. It is also important for companies that wish to install new operations or facilities that offer few employment opportunities. It is highly likely that these companies could face both regulatory and community resistance. The importance of creating income-generating opportunities in local economies has long been and will remain an important part of gaining local community support for large-scale capital investments and securing contracts with local governments.

This could also affect companies that are expected to absorb workers who are displaced. Interviewees indicated that many of the manufacturing workers who have lost their jobs due to changes in factory location most likely moved into low-skilled retail jobs or informal work. An influx of workers in these industries could change the broader dynamic between business and local stakeholders.

Assessing and mitigating the impacts of automation on communities and local economies is critically important to maintaining reputation, ensuring compliance with local laws, and contributing to prosperous local communities.

Changing Employee Engagement and Productivity

Automation has the potential to significantly increase productivity, employee communication, and engagement, particularly if linked to higher wages and opportunities to build skills and enhance mobility potential. However, capturing these gains will only happen if a conscious effort is made to address the needs and issues facing employees. At a broad level, helping workers adjust to a new work environment that is being automated will be important to maintain worker morale, engagement, and productivity.

Automation will inevitably result in some job elimination. While the amount of labor on factory floors and in agricultural production is likely to decline with widespread automation, workers will not disappear entirely. In many cases, jobs will be eliminated over time, thus affecting the morale and engagement of employees who remain, especially in cases where machines replace workmates.

Further adjustments will be required to build the skills of remaining workers, particularly if they are in limited supply in the labor market. Companies taking a thoughtful, balanced approach to reducing workforces, alongside retention strategies bolstered by technical training and upskilling, will navigate the process most effectively.

To enhance engagement and morale of remaining employees, a conscious effort should be made to share productivity gains with employees. One interviewee noted that "if you are trying to increase productivity and reduce costs, the obvious people who will suffer are the factory workers. We need to think of productivity in larger terms to keep employees happy." When productivity gains happen, there is a tendency to reinvest them in capital improvements and expect more in terms of efficiency; passing on such gains to workers in form of higher wages is less common.

Promoting Consumer Demand and Long-Term Growth

Labor-intensive manufacturing has been an important engine of economic growth for many economies. It was essential to China's economic transformation and provided a route out of poverty for millions of people. In Bangladesh, the textile and Ready-Made-Garments industry is the largest employer in the country, employing more than 3 million people, the majority of whom are women. This has played a significant role in reducing the poverty rate in the country from 56 percent in 1992 to less than 32 percent just two decades later.[12] If automation leads to a shift away from labor-intensive manufacturing and contributes to rising unemployment, there could be significant macro-level, long-term impacts on the global economy.

In its "Outlook on the Global Agenda 2015," the World Economic Forum calls out rising income inequality and persistent jobless growth as the two most important economic trends facing the global economy.[13] These factors can have a corrosive effect on the economy and on business success, partly by depressing purchasing power of the majority and undermining the tax base.[14]

This context could present significant challenges for business if total net employment declines. The International Labor Organization estimates that in the next 10 years, the world will need more than 600 million more jobs to avoid a further increase in unemployment.[15] The situation is particularly concerning for women and youth who make up the majority of the more than 200 million currently unemployed.

While technology has traditionally tended to be a net job creator, this era of technology change appears to be creating more labor-efficient industries, which limits opportunities for millions of existing and potential low-skilled workers. Automation could thus exacerbate the current economic ills, lowering aggregate demand with significant impacts on business.[16]

Viewing human capital as a cost rather than an investment could pose short- and long-term challenges for companies. At the same time, viewing automation as a way to augment and extend the capabilities of workers could make automation a win for both workers and business.

Notes

1. Davies, Anna, Devin Fidler, and Maria Gorbis. 2011. "Future Work Skills 2020." Institute for the Future. http://www.iftf.org/futureworkskills/

2. PwC. 2015. "Manufacturing Barometer April 2015. PwC. http://www.pwc.com/us/en/industrial-manufacturing/barometer-manufacturing/index.jhtml

3. McKinsey Global Institute. 2015. "Big Data: The next frontier for competition." McKinsey Global Institute. http://www.mckinsey.com/Features/Big_Data

4. Asian Development Bank. 2012. "Asia Must Close Skills Gaps, Go High Tech to Sustain Future Growth." http://www.adb.org/news/asia-must-close-skills-gaps-go-high-tech-sustain-future-growth-adb

5. Roberts, Dexter. 2013. U.S. Electronics Maker Knowles Adapts to a Changed China." Bloomberg Business. December 13. http://www.bloomberg.com/bw/articles/2013-12-19/u-dot-s-dot-electronics-maker-knowles-adapts-to-a-changed-China

6. Blanchard, Ben and Hui Li. 2014. "China taps tech training to tackle labour market mismatch." Reuters. June 8. http://in.reuters.com/article/2014/06/08/uk-china-labour-education-idINKBN0EJ01Q20140608

7. Frey, Carl Benedikt and Michael Osborne. 2015. "Technology at Work: The Future of Innovation and Employment." Oxford Martin School and Citi. http://www.oxfordmartin.ox.ac.uk/downloads/reports/Technology%20at%20Work.pdf

8. Code.org, http://code.org/promote/ca

9. The World Bank. 2013. "World Development Report 2013: Jobs." http://siteresources.worldbank.org/EXTNWDR2013/Resources/8258024-1320950747192/8260293-1322665883147/Chapter-4.pdf

10. Thompson, Derek. "A World Without Work." The Atlantic. http://www.theatlantic.com/magazine/archive/2015/07/world-without-work/395294/

11. Brynjolfsson, Erik, Andrew McAfee, and Michael Spence. 2014. "New World Order." Foreign Affairs. https://www.foreignaffairs.com/articles/united-states/2014-06-04/new-world-order

12. The World Bank. 2013. "World Development Report 2013: Jobs." http://siteresources.worldbank.org/EXTNWDR2013/Resources/8258024-

13. World Economic Forum. 2015. "Outlook on the Global Agenda 2015." http://reports.weforum.org/outlook-global-agenda-2015/

14. Davis Pluess, Jessica and Racheal Meiers. 2015. "Business Leadership for an Inclusive Economy." BSR Working Paper. http://www.bsr.org/en/our-insights/report-view/business-leadership-for-an-inclusive-economy-a-framework-for-collaboration

15. ILO. 2012. "Global Employment Trends 2012: Preventing a deeper jobs crisis." http://www.ilo.org/wcmsp5/groups/public/@dgreports/@dcomm/@publ/documents/publication/wcms_171 571.pdf

16. Frey, Carl Benedikt and Michael Osborne. 2015. "Technology at Work: The Future of Innovation and Employment." Oxford Martin School and Citi.

| "We need to prepare people to enter the large number of jobs that will be available due to the retirement of baby boomers."

Robots Won't Steal All Our Jobs as Long as Employers and Workers Adapt

Paul Osterman

In the following viewpoint, Paul Osterman argues that while certain sectors will see a decrease in job openings in the coming years, opportunities in these fields will still exist. In fact, such jobs will not be nearly as hard to come by as some reports would have the public believe. Broadening the training and scope of work for employees in many fields—like home health care, for instance—will enable a huge portion of the employed population to maintain their "employed" status, even as the ways in which automation are affecting their industries continue to grow. Osterman is the Nanyang Technological University (NTU) Professor of Human Resources and Management at the MIT Sloan School of Management, as well as a member of the Department of Urban Planning at MIT.

As you read, consider the following questions:

1. What needs to happen to jobs in order to keep them relevant as the impact of technology continues and increases?
2. What is something policy makers must focus on as automation becomes more prevalent?
3. Over what time frame does the author say "we need to prepare people to enter the large number of jobs that will be available due to the retirement of baby boomers"?

The unemployment rate may be descending towards its natural level. But that hasn't stopped many economists and workers from worrying about the future of the job market, and the long-term impacts of automation. Work is gradually disappearing, the argument goes. Robots will steal our jobs.

Of course, history is littered with moments when people worried about the impact of technology on jobs and many of those concerns proved unfounded. The current climate is no different. But our obsession with robots is leading us to overlook challenges and opportunities of much greater practical importance than worries about automation.

The opportunity lies in an oft-ignored fact: even those occupations which are contracting due to technological change will continue to provide plenty of job openings over the next two decades. The challenge lies in improving the quality of these jobs going forward.

Debates on this issue frequently overlook a key distinction between net change and the flow of job openings. Consider blue collar production jobs—the classic example of an occupation that will dramatically shrink due to technical change. In the year 2024, there will be 282,000 fewer such jobs than in 2014, according to projections by the Bureau of Labor Statistics. But does this mean that there will be no job openings in production, as some people argue? Absolutely not. Aging baby boomers will retire, creating replacement openings. Indeed, the same government projections point to 2.2 million production job openings.

This same pattern holds across the board. Overall projections of actual job openings are five times the predicted net growth in employment.

So, what does this mean? The demand for workers with new or broader skill sets is gradually rising, ensuring that the new production hire of tomorrow will need to be more capable than the person he or she will replace.

That said, my own research—based on a nationally representative survey of manufacturers—suggests that these evolving "skill demands" don't require as much education as many people believe; in fact, most in-demand skills can be obtained at the community college level. For example, three-quarters of employers in the survey said they only required basic math for their frontline workers, a skill set that can be obtained without an advanced degree. (Just 14 percent of employers said they required their employees to have an understanding of probability and statistics, and only 7 percent required knowledge of calculus.)

The lesson is that investments in our human capital make sense—and they're within reach for more people than is commonly assumed. This is a very different conclusion than the popular argument that work is ending. Instead of worrying about some future automated workforce, the nation's economic policy agenda should focus on preparing people for the large number of replacement openings that will develop in the years to come. But that's only part of the solution. Policymakers must also focus on job quality at the bottom of the labor market.

Last year, 27 percent of employees in the United States earned a wage of $13.93 an hour or less. Full-time, year-round work at that hourly wage still puts those employees below 150 percent of the poverty level for a family of three with one child. The nation's large low-wage job market is a problem, but viewed from another perspective it also represents enormous potential. Instead of anguishing over robots, why not focus on improving job quality for people who are currently employed, so they won't eventually get replaced by machines.

But while improving job quality is a crucial and much-needed next step, it's also a complicated task. We know of some proven and effective tools, such as raising the minimum wage, incentivizing decent overtime pay, and expanding unionization. But, while effective, implementing these approaches on a national level remains politically fraught. In particular, growing the unionized workforce—arguably the most effective means of ensuring better jobs—doesn't seem likely, at least in the foreseeable future.

A more promising—and perhaps realistic—strategy is to convince employers that upgrading their workers' job quality is in their own best interest. The potential policy menu for accomplishing this includes the government setting an example by insisting that its contractors provide good jobs; building job ladders so that entry work can lead to higher quality jobs; convincing Wall Street that high-road policies are profitable; and demonstrating the economic benefits of improved job quality.

My favorite example of the latter approach is in health care. Specifically, in the role of home health care aides. The sector has over two million workers today and is slated to grow even further as the baby boomer generation ages and the demand for home health care rises. Yet these direct-care workers make on average $10 per hour. The sector's workforce is almost entirely female, and most are minorities. A significant percentage of home health care aides are also immigrants. These jobs will always be with us; the robots are not an issue. The better question is, how can they be improved?

Today, these home health care aides receive minimal training and are often limited by regulations from performing a broad range of tasks. In some states they cannot even administer eye drops! The solution is to show that aides can do much more, if properly trained—a change that would have the added benefit of reducing health care costs.

For example, aides could also serve as health coaches who help clients with diabetes eat more carefully and get exercise. Health care aides could assist in transitioning patients from hospitals to their homes, thereby reducing the number of costly nursing home stays. They could also be incorporated into larger health care teams; putting home health care aides in better touch with doctors and nurses would reduce the number of unnecessary trips to the emergency room. There is good evidence that all of this is possible and if it were to happen then the payers—insurance companies and Medicaid—would save money and home health care aides could earn more.

Over the next two decades, we need to prepare people to enter the large number of jobs that will be available due to the retirement of baby boomers. This means investing in education and training for skills that are certainly attainable by the vast majority of people. And it means shrinking the scope of our large low-wage job market by convincing firms that it pays to invest in job quality improvement. By tackling these challenges, we'll be able to focus on the economy of the future, and stop worrying as much about robots stealing our jobs.

> "When we talk about robotization, we are not talking about the enormous robot at Boston University; we are talking about a self-checkout machine or an online translator."

Job Loss and Automation Are Not Necessarily Connected

The World Bank Group

In the following viewpoint, the World Bank Group interviews Ignacio Apella, an expert on social protection who argues that an "older population means a small number of people of working age and therefore a lower capacity to produce goods and services," in the context of Uruguay and Argentina. In addition, he notes that while robotization does not directly lead to the elimination of jobs, it does create a shift in the way work is done, and by whom. Essentially, while automation may lead to the replacement of some workers, those individuals' skills will be needed elsewhere to maintain productivity and keep up with the machines. The World Bank Group is a non-profit organization with 189 member countries, with the twofold mission of ending extreme poverty and promoting shared prosperity.

"Are You Afraid of Losing Your Job to Automation?" The World Bank Group, July 11, 2017. Reprinted by permission.

As you read, consider the following questions:

1. The aging population of what two countries are discussed in the article?
2. What group of workers runs the risk of being left out of the market as an increasing number of tasks becomes automated?
3. What aspect of education needs to increase in order to better prepare children for the shifting job market?

Studies and articles that warn about the impact of new technologies on jobs have become increasingly common. They range from apocalyptic assessments claiming that robots—whether these are large industrial machines or simple self-checkout machines—will eliminate thousands of jobs, to those that postulate that although automation may affect certain tasks, this new scenario will imply a shift in the acquisition of skills and a change of teaching methods to adapt to the new demands of the labor market.

What can Latin America do to prepare for this scenario?

Argentina and Uruguay have experienced a shift in the profile of employment, which has changed from labor-intensive, manual tasks to more cognitive tasks. This has resulted from the current process of technological change in both countries. The main medium-term challenge centers on tasks susceptible to automation, associated with a worrying increase in technological unemployment and the ageing of the workforce.

We asked Ignacio Apella, a World Bank expert on social protection and one of the authors of the study "Technological change and the labor market in Argentina and Uruguay: A task-centered analysis," to explain the findings from those two countries and their implications for the rest of the region.

Question. According to the report, the impact of technological change on the labor market goes beyond employment; it also affects countries with a marked ageing of the population. How is this related?

Answer. Two years ago, we began to research the economic challenges that an ageing population posed in Uruguay and Argentina. One interesting finding is that the ageing process is a limiting factor in terms of long-term economic growth. Why? Because an older population means a small number of people of working age and therefore a lower capacity to produce goods and services. A possible response to overcome this limitation is to increase labor productivity; in other words, even with a smaller working-age population, more can be produced, which can maintain GDP per capita. Following several discussions with the governments of both countries, we determined that this phenomenon is occurring with another mega-trend, which is technological change.

This has existed since the wheel was invented. The issue here is that it has been occurring more rapidly over the past 20 or 30 years. And that is a great opportunity for the countries that are experiencing an ageing process because technological change allows you to increase global productivity of the economy, which is what we want in this context. The problem is that this great opportunity also entails major challenges due to its effects on the labor market. So, with this latest study, we tried to understand those implications, the risks and technological challenges to the labor market.

Q. Robotization has a direct impact on the labor market, which requires more qualified workers. How can we address this challenge to increase labor productivity?

A. When we talk about robotization, we are not talking about the enormous robot at Boston University; we are talking about a self-checkout machine or an online translator. When we talk about robots, we are referring to physical and digital machines. Robotization does not make occupations or jobs disappear; what it replaces are tasks that workers perform in their jobs. All workers do a variety of tasks. Machines will replace some of them.

The type of tasks that automation may replace or substitute are those characterized as routine, that have a defined set of actions that are invariably repeated and that make them susceptible to becoming automated. The risk to the labor market is the reduction in employment for these types of routine tasks. Particularly manual tasks, although cognitive ones are not exempt, in other words, those that require knowledge. In this case, I give the example of translators. The occupation is that of the translator and one of the tasks translators perform is to identify the phrase, its grammatical structure, and to translate it. This is a cognitive but routine task. An online translator can perform this task. Digital translators now do a much better job than they did 10 years ago because they are learning patterns of behavior, which are incorporated by their users. Thus, both manual and cognitive routine tasks are at risk.

Q. What are the recommendations to address this issue and how can we guarantee that a country with an ageing working-age population is sufficiently prepared to take advantage of technological change?

A. Technological change is welcome because it enables increases in the productivity of the economy and thus generates the capacity for growth, but it can increase inequality in income distribution —unlike the first industrial revolution. The labor market runs the risk of becoming polarized. This means that two groups of workers will remain: those who are highly skilled and who perform tasks that are not susceptible to automation, in other words, non-routine, cognitive tasks (which require critical thinking, problem-solving, creativity, innovation, interpersonal relations) and which are associated with high income. At the other extreme is the group of less qualified workers who perform tasks that are market remnants, in general, non-routine, manual tasks that are not susceptible to being automated but that generate less income. In the middle, workers of medium skills and income run the risk of being left out of the market. This is where the middle class is, which is employed in the service and manufacturing sectors. Based on this assessment, there are two major challenges, one short-term and the other medium- and long-term but that requires immediate action, especially considering the speed at which this technological change is occurring.

In the short term, the first risk is the technological unemployment that could be generated. Here there are two public policy alternatives to be evaluated: the first is restriction, in other words, protecting those sectors that are intensive in automation-susceptible tasks so that automation does not penetrate those sectors and therefore does not replace workers. In light of the continuous technological change, the effort needed will be continuous, as will the costs of the intervention. It has been done, there are actors in power that play and pressure and have some type of influence, but I don't think this is an effective option in the short term. Alternatively,—and I think it is more efficient—we can improve all continuing education programs, which teach skills to young adults to enable them to adapt to the new working conditions and to perform other types of tasks that they were not familiar with.

In the long term, given that all change generates new occupations, which we cannot predict, the challenge is that we do not know how to educate today's children. We believe that it is worth rethinking the three levels of the education system —early childhood, primary and secondary—as a whole to try to determine the relevance of what is being taught and to improve the system through which it is delivered and knowledge is acquired. We need to switch from a rote learning system to one of more critical analysis. Children are still required to memorize when we actually have a 1-terabyte hard disk with more memory capacity than our own. That is the discussion we should be having. It's difficult because there are actors in the game who react, but I think it's a debate that should be put on the table.

Periodical and Internet Sources Bibliography

The following articles have been selected to supplement the diverse views presented in this chapter.

David Autor and Anna Salomons, "Is Automation Labor-Displacing? Productivity, growth, employment, and the labor share," *Brookings Papers on Economic Activity,* March 8–9, 2018. brookings.edu/wp-content/uploads/2018/03/1_autorsalomons .pdf.

Carl Benedikt Frey and Michael A. Osborne, "The Future of Employment: How susceptible are jobs to computerization?," ScienceDirect, January 2017. sciencedirect.com/science/article /pii/S0040162516302244.

Nick Heath, "AI Will Destroy Entry-Level Jobs—But Lead to a Basic Income for All," TechRepublic, May 5, 2016. techrepublic.com /article/ai-will-destroy-entry-level-jobs-but-lead-to-a-basic -income-for-all.

Lucy Ingham, "Stephen Hawking: 'The Rise of AI Will Be Either the Best or Worst Thing Ever to Happen to Humanity,'" Factor, March 14, 2018. factor-tech.com/feature/stephen-hawking-the -rise-of-powerful-ai-will-be-either-the-best-or-the-worst-thing -ever-to-happen-to-humanity.

Daniel Kuehn, "Automation's Effects on Jobs Are More Complicated Than You Might Think," Urban Institute, February 19, 2018. urban.org/urban-wire/automations-effects-jobs-are-more -complicated-you-might-think.

James Manyinka, Jaana Remes, Jan Mischke, and Mikala Krishnan, "New Insights into the Slowdown in US Productivity Growth," McKinsey Global Institute, March 2017, mckinsey.com/featured -insights/employment-and-growth/new-insights-into-the -slowdown-in-us-productivity-growth.

NCCI, "The Impact of Automation on Employment—Part 1," NCCI, October 10, 2017. https://www.ncci.com/Articles/Pages/II_ Insights_QEB_Impact-Automation-Employment-Q2-2017-Part1. aspx.

David Rotman, "How Technology Is Destroying Jobs," MIT Technology Review, June 12, 2013. technologyreview .com/s/515926/how-technology-is-destroying-jobs.

Rachael Stephens, "Robots at Work: The economic effects of workplace automation," Journalist's Resource, September 22, 2015. journalistsresource.org/studies/economics/jobs/robots-at-work-the-economics-effects-of-workplace-automation.

Andrew Stettner, "Mounting a Response to Technological Unemployment," The Century Foundation, April 26, 2018. tcf.org /content/report/mounting-response-technological -unemployment/?agreed=1.

Chapter 2

Is Resistance to the Automation of Labor Just a Present-Day Version of the Luddite Fallacy?

Chapter Preface

In addition to the potential challenges faced by entry-level workers trying to find jobs, the automation of labor can also result in already-employed people losing their jobs. Some industries or entire fields of employment are being eliminated as a result of automation. From EZ-Pass technology replacing toll collectors, to 3D printing completing the work that many used to do by hand, to self-driving cars potentially replacing the need for drivers, evidence exists to prove that this is a real concern.

However, some elements of cause and effect are at work here. Changes like the ones described above may contribute to cost savings for consumers at large. With that in mind, people's willingness to spend money on experiences may create a demand for more employees in businesses in those industries, which will thrive as a result. Examples of industries where this kind of growth is likely include tourism, such as family trips, individual getaways, social gatherings for a weekend away, self-care, and 3D movies.

The viewpoints in the following chapter debate whether or not society should panic at the thought of such changes to the workforce and economy. One author, for example, predicts mass unemployment at the hands of automation and artificial intelligence while another argues that a need for human employees will remain, and that education and public policy will play prominent roles in the proper handling of the changes to come. Should we take comfort in the notion that jobs have been automated for a long time and the workforce has been reshaped—and survived—before, or should we be thrust into action at the frightening thought that we are headed for trouble?

| "*Our current economy and society will transform in significant ways, with no simple fixes or adaptations to lessen their effects.*"

Look to the Industrial Revolution to Understand How Painful the Transition to Automation Will Be

Moshe Y. Vardi

In the following viewpoint, Moshe Y. Vardi argues that the future of automation is a force to be reckoned with and that mass unemployment will result from technological change. He notes that automation and artificial intelligence are pervading entire economies and that professionals including accountants, lawyers, truckers, and even construction workers should be wary of such changes. Vardi offers a warning that historical perspective is important and should be taken into account as we move into the future. Vardi is a professor of computer science at Rice University.

"What the Industrial Revolution Really Tells Us About the Future of Automation and Work," by Moshe Y. Vardi, The Conversation, September 2, 2017. https://theconversation .com/what-the-industrial-revolution-really-tells-us-about-the-future-of-automation-and -work-82051. Licensed under CC BY-ND 4.0 International.

As you read, consider the following questions:

1. Between 1995 and 2015, what was the impact
   of technology replacing workers on U.S.
   manufacturing productivity?
2. What did the Association for Computing Machinery
   conclude about computer industry jobs as they related to
   developed countries?
3. What vote in the U.K. does the author consider to have
   been driven in large part by economic grievances?

As automation and artificial intelligence technologies improve, many people worry about the future of work. If millions of human workers no longer have jobs, the worriers ask, what will people do, how will they provide for themselves and their families, and what changes might occur (or be needed) in order for society to adjust?

Many economists say there is no need to worry. They point to how past major transformations in work tasks and labor markets —specifically the Industrial Revolution during the 18th and 19th centuries—did not lead to major social upheaval or widespread suffering. These economists say that when technology destroys jobs, people find other jobs. As one economist argued:

> Since the dawn of the industrial age, a recurrent fear has been that technological change will spawn mass unemployment. Neoclassical economists predicted that this would not happen, because people would find other jobs, albeit possibly after a long period of painful adjustment. By and large, that prediction has proven to be correct.

They are definitely right about the long period of painful adjustment! The aftermath of the Industrial Revolution involved two major Communist revolutions, whose death toll approaches 100 million. The stabilizing influence of the modern social welfare state emerged only after World War II, nearly 200 years on from the 18th-century beginnings of the Industrial Revolution.

Today, as globalization and automation dramatically boost corporate productivity, many workers have seen their wages stagnate. The increasing power of automation and artificial intelligence technology means more pain may follow. Are these economists minimizing the historical record when projecting the future, essentially telling us not to worry because in a century or two things will get better?

Reaching a Tipping Point

To learn from the Industrial Revolution, we must put it in the proper historical context. The Industrial Revolution was a tipping point. For many thousands of years before it, economic growth was practically negligible, generally tracking with population growth: Farmers grew a bit more food and blacksmiths made a few more tools, but people from the early agrarian societies of Mesopotamia, Egypt, China and India would have recognized the world of 17th-century Europe.

But when steam power and industrial machinery came along in the 18th century, economic activity took off. The growth that happened in just a couple hundred years was on a vastly different scale than anything that had happened before. We may be at a similar tipping point now, referred to by some as the "Fourth Industrial Revolution," where all that has happened in the past may appear minor compared to the productivity and profitability potential of the future.

Getting Predictions Wrong

It is easy to underestimate in advance the impact of globalization and automation—I have done it myself. In March 2000, the NASDAQ Composite Index peaked and then crashed, wiping out US$8 trillion in market valuations over the next two years. At the same time, the global spread of the internet enabled offshore outsourcing of software production, leading to fears of information technology jobs disappearing en masse.

The Association for Computing Machinery worried what these factors might mean for computer education and employment in the future. Its study group, which I co-chaired, reported in 2006 that there was no real reason to believe that computer industry jobs were migrating away from developed countries. The last decade has vindicated that conclusion.

Our report conceded, however, that "trade gains may be distributed differentially," meaning some individuals and regions would gain and others would lose. And it was focused narrowly on the information technology industry. Had we looked at the broader impact of globalization and automation on the economy, we might have seen the much bigger changes that even then were taking hold.

Spreading to Manufacturing

In both the first Industrial Revolution and today's, the first effects were in manufacturing in the developed world. By substituting technology for workers, U.S. manufacturing productivity roughly doubled between 1995 and 2015. As a result, while U.S. manufacturing output today is essentially at an all-time high, employment peaked around 1980, and has been declining precipitously since 1995.

Unlike in the 19th century, though, the effects of globalization and automation are spreading across the developing world. Economist Branko Milanovic's "Elephant Curve" shows how people around the globe, ranked by their income in 1998, saw their incomes increase by 2008. While the income of the very poor was stagnant, rising incomes in emerging economies lifted hundreds of millions of people out of poverty. People at the very top of the income scale also benefited from globalization and automation.

But the income of working- and middle-class people in the developed world has stagnated. In the U.S., for example, income of production workers today, adjusted for inflation, is essentially at the level it was around 1970.

Now automation is also coming to developing-world economies. A recent report from the International Labor Organization found that more than two-thirds of Southeast Asia's 9.2 million textile and footwear jobs are threatened by automation.

Waking Up to the Problems

In addition to spreading across the world, automation and artificial intelligence are beginning to pervade entire economies. Accountants, lawyers, truckers and even construction workers —whose jobs were largely unchanged by the first Industrial Revolution—are about to find their work changing substantially, if not entirely taken over by computers.

Until very recently, the global educated professional class didn't recognize what was happening to working- and middle-class people in developed countries. But now it is about to happen to them.

The results will be startling, disruptive and potentially long-lasting. Political developments of the past year make it clear that the issue of shared prosperity cannot be ignored. It is now evident that the Brexit vote in the U.K. and the election of President Donald Trump in the U.S. were driven to a major extent by economic grievances.

Our current economy and society will transform in significant ways, with no simple fixes or adaptations to lessen their effects. But when trying to make economic predictions based on the past, it is worth remembering—and exercising—the caution provided by the distinguished Israeli economist Ariel Rubinstein in his 2012 book, "Economic Fables":

> I am obsessively occupied with denying any interpretation contending that economic models produce conclusions of real value.

Rubinstein's basic assertion, which is that economic theory tells us more about economic models than it tells us about economic reality, is a warning: We should listen not only to economists when it comes to predicting the future of work; we should listen also to historians, who often bring a deeper historical perspective to their predictions. Automation will significantly change many people's lives in ways that may be painful and enduring.

"Young people will bear the brunt of AI-fueled job losses as smart systems undercut entry-level roles in everything from marketing to retail."

Disruption in the Job Market Already Has Begun

Nick Heath

In the following viewpoint, Nick Heath argues that job losses that happen as a result of advances in AI will be felt most strongly by younger people. He points to the statistics about the automation of jobs in the near future, particularly as they relate to entry-level work. He also discusses the still-emerging gig economy and draws connections to this and the reduction in full-time employees in exchange for contracted work. Heath also points to expert advice that, to see benefits of AI, it's important to scale the length of time for system training. Heath is chief reporter for TechRepublic.

As you read, consider the following questions:

1. At what level are the jobs are being reduced by AI?
2. What type of economy sees people contracting small tasks on demand?
3. Name two areas where companies are looking into automating roles that have traditionally been manual.

Young people will bear the brunt of AI-fueled job losses as smart systems undercut entry-level roles in everything from marketing to retail.

Machine learning and expert systems will not destroy jobs wholesale, predicts George Zarkadakis, digital lead at advisory firm Willis Towers Watson, but will remove the need for many tasks that employees have traditionally cut their teeth on at the beginning of their careers.

Zarkadakis cited a study by consultants McKinsey, which found that just under one third of activities that make up 60 percent of existing jobs will be automated.

Unfortunately for new entrants to job markets, the bulk of these activities will be concentrated in starter roles, said Zarkadakis.

"We've done some research ourselves and looked at the impact on entry-level jobs. Jobs that graduates get once they leave university. We found that many of the entry-level jobs are very susceptible to complete obliteration," he told The AI Summit in London.

"But look at the impact. What will happen to the world when young graduates will not be able to enter the job market? There will be major disruption in the labor market."

The automation of these activities will cut about $1tn from business' wage bills, predicts Zarkadakis, good news for companies he said, but potentially bad for workers.

In the future, increasing numbers of people will work in the so-called "gig economy," Zarkadakis claimed, where companies contract individuals to perform small tasks on demand. This type of work differs from full time employment in that there are no guarantees of long term ties between the employer and employee—with fewer obligations on both sides.

"This sort of disruption in the job market is already happening because of the gig economy and if we want to have an idea about what will happen with AI, we only need to see what's already happening with digital platforms," he said.

"Increasingly companies are reducing full time employees and using those digital platforms to acquire the desired skills on a contract basis. Maybe that's telling of what the future will be like."

This shift away from steady employment and income could see governments assume a greater role in preventing individuals from slipping into poverty.

"We'll have people being responsible for their financial well-being, as opposed to companies looking after them. The role of government will be increased, probably through universal income," he said, citing experiments with schemes to guarantee everybody a basic income in various countries worldwide.

Yet Zarkadakis' is only one point of view, Microsoft's chief envisioning officer Dave Coplin, expressed frustration at talk of technology destroying jobs, pointing out that technology generally complements human labor, rather than replaces it.

"We're locked in this endless cycle of pointless rhetoric of humans vs machines," said Coplin, whose employer offers a range of machine learning services via Microsoft Azure cloud and is pushing the idea of smart bots powered by its Cortana virtual assistant as the future of customer relations.

"'Machines can beat us at chess, they can beat us at Go, they're going to steal our jobs'. Hang on. Stop. When was this ever the dialogue for what we did with technology? Technology is here to augment what we do."

Roadblocks to Widespread Automation

Beyond the question of how AI will affect society, there is the more practical consideration of how long it will be before the technology is mature enough to affect such changes.

Companies are beginning to look at using machine learning and expert systems to further automate manual roles in service industries, in areas ranging from handling helpdesk calls to training shop assistants.

But Harrick Vin, chief scientist at Indian outsourcer Tata Consultancy Services, highlighted the significant obstacles to training machine learning systems that, until solved, will hamper the use of such systems to replace manual labor.

Training machines using supervised learning can take six to 18 months for every new domain of knowledge—an issue when each business can have many different domains they are seeking to automate—he said.

"If you really want to see benefits, like the ones that are being projected, then you've got to figure out how to scale and not take six months, one year, 18 months to train an engine to perform one task, because a typical large business performs hundreds, if not thousands, of different activities."

Without reducing this upfront training time, "it is going to be impossible to scale," he said.

And not only does it take too long to train systems, once ready to use such systems will likely need new training as businesses change the data they collect and the way they do business.

"You have to build these systems to be inherently adaptable," he said.

> "Having 'disrupted' industries
> including manufacturing, music,
> journalism and retail, Silicon Valley
> has its eyes on trucking."

The American Trucking Industry Sees Automation in Its Future

Dominic Rushe

In the following viewpoint, Dominic Rushe argues that automation is already part of the trucking industry and that it's only a matter of time before the industry is far more—if not fully—automated. The author tells the story of a career truck driver who is afraid of the possibility of losing his job for this reason. However, he counters this story with a show of confidence from the world's largest truck stop, which continues to grow. Rushe also looks ahead to potential perceptions of the current state of the trucking industry and how today's statistics will be received by future generations. Rushe is the business editor for Guardian US.

"Will Automation Put an End to the American Trucker?" by Dominic Rushe, Guardian News and Media Limited, October 10, 2017. Reprinted by permission.

As you read, consider the following questions:

1. Which two states have passed laws allowing trucks to drive autonomously in "platoons" of two or more big rigs driving together?
2. What union pushed Congress to slow legislation on broadening the use of autonomous vehicles?
3. What are some of the arguments the author anticipates from people in the future, about the benefits of autonomous trucks?

Jeff Baxter's sunflower-yellow Kenworth truck shines as bright and almost as big as the sun. Four men clean the glistening cab in the hangar-like truck wash at Iowa 80, the world's largest truck stop.

Baxter has made a pitstop at Iowa 80 before picking up a 116 ft-long wind turbine blade that he's driving down to Texas, 900 miles away.

Baxter, 48, is one of the 1.8 million Americans, mainly men, who drive heavy trucks for a living, the single most common job in many US states. Driving is one of the biggest occupations in the world. Another 1.7 million people drive taxis, buses and delivery vehicles in the US alone. But for how long? Having "disrupted" industries including manufacturing, music, journalism and retail, Silicon Valley has its eyes on trucking.

Google, Uber, Tesla and the major truck manufacturers are looking to a future in which people like Baxter will be replaced—or at the very least downgraded to co-pilots—by automated vehicles that will save billions but will cost millions of jobs. It will be one of the biggest changes to the jobs market since the invention of the automated loom—challenging the livelihoods of millions across the world.

"I'm scared to death of that," says Baxter, an impish man with bad teeth that he hides behind his hand as he laughs. "I can't operate a pocket calculator!"

But Baxter is in the minority. Iowa 80 is a great place to check the pulse of the trucking community. Interstate 80—the second longest in the country—runs from downtown San Francisco to the edge of New York City. The truck stop, about 40 miles east of Iowa City, serves 5,000 customers each day, offering everything they could need from shops and restaurants to a cinema, chiropractor, dentist, barber and a chapel.

Every week, a major tech company seems to announce some new development in automated trucking. Next month, the Tesla founder, Elon Musk, will unveil an electric-powered semi that is likely to be semi-autonomous. But most of the truckers I spoke to were not concerned by the rise of the robots. "I don't think a robot could do my job," says Ray Rodriguez, 38, who has driven up a batch of cars from Tennessee. "Twenty years from now, maybe."

Nor do the managers of the Iowa 80 see their jobs changing any time soon. "The infrastructure just isn't there," says Heather DeBaillie, marketing manager of Iowa 80. Nor does she think that people are ready for autonomous trucks. "Think about the airplane. They could automate an airplane now. So why don't they have airplanes without pilots?" She also argues that the politics of laying off so many people will not pass muster in Washington.

The family-run Iowa 80 has been serving truckers for 53 years, and is so confident about its future that it is expanding to secure its claim to being the world's biggest truck stop, adding more restaurants and shopping space to the "Disneyland of truckers."

But not everyone is so confident that truck stops will survive the age of the algorithm. Finn Murphy, author of *The Long Haul*, the story of his life as a long-distance truck driver, says the days of the truck driver as we know him are coming to an end. Trucking is a $700bn industry, in which a third of costs go to compensating drivers, and, he says, if the tech firms can grab a slice of that, they will.

"The only human beings left in the modern supply chain are truck drivers. If you go to a modern warehouse now, say Amazon or Walmart, the trucks are unloaded by machines, the trucks are

THE IMPACT OF AUTONOMOUS VEHICLES

While the Department of Commerce is pessimistic about the impact of autonomous vehicles on the job prospects of the older, less educated people who tend to work as motor vehicle operators, they are bullish about how the new technology will affect on-the-job drivers. They may "benefit from greater productivity and better working conditions," the report claims. The use of autonomous vehicles could actually increase the demand for certain jobs by reducing their costs. For example, plumbers and electricians may become cheaper because of lower transport costs, and because those workers will be able use that travel time to manage their billing or prepare for their next appointment.

The Department of Commerce also points out that even if some of these on-the-job drivers are displaced, they will probably be able to find other work that makes sense for them. Compared to motor vehicle operators, these people tend to be more educated, and currently in jobs that call for the kind of problem-solving skills that are most in demand in the labor market. They also tend to be younger and thus, on the whole, more adaptable.

The Department of Commerce's report is a reminder of the complex ways that autonomous vehicles will impact the future of work. Yes, truck drivers will probably be replaced and commutes will be more pleasant because you'll be able to watch TV. But not needing to drive will also change the work of police officers and electricians in ways we can't foresee.

"Driverless Cars Will Make a Lot of Jobs Better, Not Destroy Them," by Dan Kopf, Quartz Media LLC, August 25, 2017.

loaded by machines, they are put into the warehouse by machines. Then there is a guy, probably making $10 an hour, with a load of screens watching these machines. Then what you have is a truckers' lounge with 20 or 30 guys standing around getting paid. And that drives the supply chain people nuts," he says.

The goal, he believes, is to get rid of the drivers and "have ultimate efficiency."

"I think this is imminent. Five years or so. This is a space race—the race to get the first driverless vehicle that is viable," says Murphy. "My fellow drivers don't appear to be particularly concerned about this. They think it's way off into the future. All the people I have talked to on this book tour, nobody thinks this is imminent except for me. Me and Elon Musk, I guess."

The future is coming. Arguably it is already here. Several states have already laid the groundwork for a future with fewer truckers. California, Florida, Michigan and Utah have passed laws allowing trucks to drive autonomously in "platoons," where two or more big rigs drive together and synchronize their movements.

The stage has been set for a battle between the forces of labor and the tech titans. In July, the powerful Teamsters union successfully pushed Congress to slow legislation for states looking to broaden the use of autonomous vehicles. After arm-twisting by the union, the US House of Representatives energy and commerce committee exempted vehicles over 10,000lb from new rules meant to speed the development of autonomous cars. Many truckers came into the industry after being displaced by automation in other industries, and the transportation secretary, Elaine Chao, has said she is "very concerned" about the impact of self-driving cars on US jobs.

But Ryan Petersen sees the Teamsters' move as a speed bump at best. Petersen, the founder of Flexport, a tech-savvy freight logistics company, says fully operational self-driving trucks will start replacing jobs within the next year, and will probably become commonplace within 10.

"Labor accounts for 75% of the cost of transporting shipments by truck, so adopters can begin to realize those savings. Beyond that, while truckers are prohibited from driving more than 11 hours per day without taking an eight-hour break, a driverless truck can drive for the entire day. This effectively doubles the output of the trucking network at a quarter of the cost. That's an eight-times increase in productivity, without taking into account other benefits gained by automation," he says.

Larger trucks making highway trips, like those occupying the 900-truck parking spots at Iowa 90, are the lowest-hanging fruit and will be automated first, Petersen says.

Last year, Otto, a self-driving truck company owned by Uber, successfully delivered 45,000 cans of Budweiser in a truck that drove the 130-odd miles from Fort Collins, Colorado, to Colorado Springs. A semi-automated platoon of trucks crossed Europe last year in an experiment coordinated by DAF, Daimler, Iveco, MAN, Scania and Volvo.

But the automation that seems to most concern drivers at Iowa 80 concerns their log books. Truck firms are shifting drivers over to computerized logs—and they hate it. The new system adds another layer of oversight to an industry that is already heavily regulated, and will limit where and when drivers can stop. A driver looking to add an extra 30 minutes to his ride in order to make it to the truck stop rather than rest up in a layby might find that option gone, under a system that is centrally controlled rather than filled in by him in the log books that occupy a long shelf in Iowa 80's giant trucker store.

The trucker holds a special place in American mythology: sometimes a symbol of freedom and the open road, sometimes a threat. Truckers entered popular culture from all directions, from the existential horror of Spielberg's *Duel*, to *Convoy*, the bizarre trucker protest song that became a global hit and introduced the world to CB radio slang—Let them truckers roll, 10-4!"

In the 1970s, Hollywood's he-men wanted to be truckers: Kris Kristofferson in *Convoy*, inspired by the song; Burt Reynolds CB-slanging his way through S*mokey and the Bandit* I and II. *Thelma and Louise* took their revenge on a cat-calling trucker in 1991. Hollywood, presciently, had a cyborg drive a big rig in *Terminator 2*, and went full robot with Optimus Prime in the *Transformers* franchise. At the turn of the 21st century, the ever nostalgic hipsters' love of trucker hats and T-shirts revived America's fetishization of the long-distance driver.

But it's a nostalgia out of sync with a reality of declining wages, thanks in part to declining union powers, restricted freedoms, and a job under mortal threat from technology, says Murphy. Truckers made an average of $38,618 a year in 1980. If wages had just kept pace with inflation, that would be over $114,722 today—but last year the average wage was $41,340.

"The myth is that the long-haul truck driver is the cultural evolution of the free-range cowboy from the 19th century," says Murphy. "In fact, trucking is one of the most regulated industries in the United States. Every move the trucker makes is tracked by a computer. We have logs we need to keep every time we stop, pull over, take a leak. The truck's speed, braking, acceleration is all recorded. This is not a cowboy on the open range. This is more like 1984 than 1894."

Douglas Barry has been driving trucks since 1990. A wiry firecracker of a man, Barry says those pushing for automation are failing to see the bigger picture. The general public is just not ready to see 80,000lb of 18-wheeler flying down the highway with no one at the wheel.

"That big old rig could blow sky-high, slam into a school. It needs a human being. There isn't a machine that can equal a human being," he says. "Artificial intelligence can be hacked ... Who is ready for that? I wouldn't want my family going down the road next to a truck that's computer-operated."

He says the involvement of the tech companies has stopped people from looking for more holistic solutions to transportation problems. The answer is better roads, more delivery points for trains, streamlining the supply system—not just looking for ways of cutting manpower.

"A lot of these people at Google and so forth are very intelligent. But in a lot of ways they are out of touch with reality," Barry says.

Yet computers don't get tired, don't drink or take drugs, and don't get distracted or get road rage. Murphy, the author, says the argument that people are better than machines will not hold for long—especially as more and more people get used to autonomous cars.

"The assumption is that we are living in some kind of driver utopia now and machines are going to destroy that," he says. "The fact is that we have 41,000 highway deaths in America every year. If we piled those bodies up, that would be a public health crisis. But we are so used to the 41,000 deaths that we don't even think about it."

Virtually all those deaths are from driver error, he says. "What if we took that number down to 200? Here's how it looks to me. Thirty years from now my grandchildren are going to say to me: 'You people had pedals on machines that you slowed down and sped up with? You had a wheel to turn it? And everybody had their own? And you were killing 41,000 people a year? You people were savages!'

"They are going to look at driver-operated vehicles the way people now look at a pregnant woman smoking," he says. "It'll be the absolute epitome of barbarism."

It will also be a change in the workplace of historic proportions. "I watch a lot of Star Trek," says Baxter, as he prepares to get back on the road. "The inventions of an innovative mind can accomplish a lot of things. I just don't want to see automated trucks coming down the road in my lifetime."

| "*Will the jobs where humans have comparative advantage pay well and have good working conditions?*"

Automation and AI Can Coexist with Paying Jobs

Lori G. Kletzer

In the following viewpoint, Lori G. Kletzer argues that while automation and AI are most definitely replacing humans for many tasks and yes, even jobs, the need for real people will remain, making it unnecessary to respond to automation with the fear of the Luddites of the early 19th century. The author points to education and proper handling of public policy as tools and approaches that will properly anticipate and address achievement and opportunity gaps so the entry level workforce is appropriately prepared. Jobs that require "people" skills, such as creativity and mobility, are the most likely to remain in the hands of humans. Kletzer is the vice provost and dean of graduate studies at University of California Santa Cruz.

"The Question with AI Isn't Whether We'll Lose Our Jobs—It's How Much We'll Get Paid," by Lori G. Kletzer, Harvard Business School Publishing, January 31, 2018. Reprinted by permission.

As you read, consider the following questions:

1. What were the Luddites afraid of?
2. In what field does the Bureau of Labor Statistics say 11 of the top 25 fastest-growing occupations are?
3. What two areas of action does the author identify as being critical in preparing for a wave of automation?

The fear that machines will replace human labor is a durable one in the public mind, from the time of the Luddites in the early 19th century. Yet most economists have viewed "the end of humans in jobs" as a groundless fear, inconsistent with the evidence. The standard view of technical change is that some jobs are displaced by the substitution of machines for labor, but that the fear of total displacement is misplaced because new jobs are created, largely due to the technology-fueled increase in productivity. Humans have always shifted away from work suitable for machines and to other jobs. This was true in the 1930s, when the shift was away from agriculture, through the 1990s and early 2000s, when the shift was largely out of manufacturing.

However, the expansion of what can be automated in recent years has raised the question: Is this time different?

It doesn't have to be. Yes, there are reasons for concern, both technical and political. Machines are now able to take on less-routine tasks, and this transition is occurring during an era in which many workers are already struggling. Nonetheless, with the right policies we can get the best of both worlds: automation without rampant unemployment.

Is This Time Different?

To date, automation has meant industrial robots and computer hardware and software designed to do predictable, routine, and codifiable tasks requiring physical strength and exertion, and the repetition of logical tasks, such as calculation. With robotics, artificial intelligence, and machine learning, what we call automation seems poised to take on a greater share of high-productivity jobs and a range of tasks that were previously the domain of humans. These are tasks requiring problem solving, decision making, and interaction within a less-than-fully-predictable environment. Automation of this sort includes self-driving cars and diagnosing disease.

Automation anxiety is made more acute by a labor market that has tilted against workers over the last 30 years, with increasing income inequality and stagnant real wages. Wage growth has not kept up with productivity growth; labor's share of GDP has fallen and capital's share has risen. The social contract established after World War II, where hard work and loyalty to the firm were met with rising wages, benefits, skills training, and economic security from firms no longer characterizes much of the American workplace. The "fissured workplace"—where firms focus on their core competencies and contract out everything else—results in low pay, few benefits, and job insecurity for workers. The share of workers in alternative work arrangements, as independent contractors, franchisees, and in the gig economy, is growing substantially, from 10.7% in 2005 to 15.8% in 2015. The old structures of the postwar labor market are not up to the task of the 21st–century wave of automation, particularly for the low- and middle-skill workers already disadvantaged by previous skill-biased technological change and globalization. While technology and globalization have spurred competition, efficiency, and dynamism, the gains have not been shared by all. The unequal distribution of the gains is not a technical destiny; it is the work of institutions, business, and governments.

Will Robots Take All the Jobs?

Currently, most automation involves routine, structured, predictable physical activities and the collection and processing of data. Generally, these tasks form the basis of occupations in manufacturing, professional and business services, food service, and retail trade. Looking ahead, these tasks will continue to have the highest potential for advanced automation. Currently, less than 5% of occupations are entirely automated, and about 60% of occupations have at least 30% of tasks that can be automated. Based on these estimates, there is considerable potential for the spread of advanced automation. What is less knowable is how many new jobs will be created by automation-related productivity growth and how humans and machines will work together.

It's likely that humans will continue to dominate machines in a variety of skills, including creativity, interpersonal relations, caring, emotional range and complexity, dexterity, mobility. Luckily, we know there will be ample opportunities in these jobs. The Bureau of Labor Statistics issues periodic occupational growth projections, and in its most recent report, for the time period 2016 to 2026, 11 of the top 25 fastest-growing occupations are health care–related, where human-dominant skills are essential. These occupations include home health aides, personal care aides, physician assistants, nurse practitioners, physical therapy assistants, and aides. Some of these occupations require a four-year degree and post-baccalaureate training (nurse practitioners, physician assistants), but some require on-the-job training and certification with a high school diploma (home health aides, personal care aides, physical therapy aides).

However, even though jobs where humans have absolute advantage may be narrowing, there is little reason to expect an end to human work. The reason stems from a classic idea in economics: comparative advantage.

Even in a world where robots have absolute advantage in everything—meaning robots can do everything more efficiently than humans can—robots will be deployed where they have the greatest relative productivity advantage. Humans, meanwhile, will work where they have the smallest disadvantage. If robots can produce 10 times as many automobiles per day as a team of humans, but only twice as many houses, it makes sense to have the robots specialize and focus full-time where they're relatively most efficient, in order to maximize output. Therefore, even though

WE SIMPLY DON'T KNOW

A new NBER paper by Daron Acemoglu and Pascual Restrepo finds that "deployment of robots reduces employment and wages, but they caution that it is difficult to measure net labor market effects."

Cities with auto factories such as Detroit and Lansing have above average robot adoption and below average employment growth (actually negative.)

This study reminded me of the 2016 Autor, Dorn and Hanson study of the impact of Chinese trade on local labor markets. Even the time period was the same (1990–2007). As with robots, automation reduces employment in local markets, but this does not tell us much of anything about the effect on aggregate employment. Workers losing jobs in Detroit might migrate to Texas, where jobs are plentiful.

Do we have any evidence of the effect of trade and automation on total employment? Let's look at the unemployment rate from 1990 to 2007 (both were peak years of the business cycle.)

The unemployment rate fell slightly during this 17-year period, and thus provides no evidence that either trade or automation negatively impacted employment. However the unemployment rate is only one indicator, and many people prefer the employment to population (above age 16) ratio.

The employment ratio was about the same in 2007 as in 1990, and hence the aggregate data shows no evidence that either trade or automation reduced employment during the period studied by Autor, Card and Hanson, as well as Acemoglu and Restrepo.

Of course that doesn't mean these factors have not had a negative effect on overall employment, just that doing so would require a very sophisticated study. Unfortunately, the science of economics has not yet advanced to the point where that sort of study is feasible. And thus we are forced to admit that we simply don't know if there is any effect on overall employment.

But I do think that we know that trade and automation raise real GDP.

"Do Robots Reduce Employment?" by Scott Sumner, Liberty Fund people are a bit worse than robots at building houses, that job still falls to humans.

That means that the relevant question is "Will the jobs where humans have comparative advantage pay well and have good working conditions?" As we know from displacement due to globalization and increasing international trade, there is nothing that guarantees that humans displaced from jobs will be reemployed in new jobs that pay as well as their old jobs, or even pay well enough to maintain middle-class status.

What We Can Do

Though there is still much we don't know about how this wave of automation will proceed, there are several areas of action we can identify now.

Education and training are at the top of the list. Human capital investment must be at the center of any strategy for producing skills that are complementary to technology. The current workforce—including the unemployed—needs opportunities for re-skilling and up-skilling, with businesses taking an active role both in determining the skills needed and in providing the skill training. Workers need opportunities for lifelong learning, and employers will be key. An extensive research literature documents the high returns to workers and firms from employer-based training. Workplace training helps bridge gaps between school learning and the application of these skills in the workplace and to specific occupations.

Schools will have to change too. Anticipating future skill needs and demands adds to the urgency of addressing the many challenges in K-12 and higher education, including achievement and opportunity gaps by race and socioeconomic status in K-12 schooling, and improving access, affordability, and success in post-secondary education. The education system must also do more to produce STEM workers and to ensure that workforce is diverse.

But education alone will not be sufficient. Policy makers should focus on cushioning the necessary transitions following job loss by strengthening the social safety net. In the U.S., this means strengthening unemployment insurance (ensuring benefit adequacy, including durations of eligibility), Medicaid, Supplemental Nutrition Assistance Program, and Transitional Assistance to Needy Families. A wage insurance program for all displaced workers will help encourage people to remain attached to the labor force.

In 1966 the final report of the National Commission on Technology, Automation and Economic Progress stated, "Constant displacement is the price of a dynamic economy. History suggests that it is a price worth paying. But the accompanying burdens and benefits should be distributed fairly, and this has not always been the case." The Commission recommended responses that manage the overall health of the economy (managing and strengthening aggregate demand), promote educational opportunity, provide public employment, and secure transitional income maintenance. Fifty years later, these areas remain the basic road map for public policy response. The solutions, and any obstacles, are political, not economic or technical.

> *"It is a fantasy to believe that the wealth created by the fourth Industrial Revolution will cascade down from rich to poor, and that those displaced will just walk into another job that pays just as well."*

The Industrial Revolution 4.0 Is Cause for Concern

Larry Elliott

In the following viewpoint, Larry Elliott argues that the latest wave of innovation, while focused on groundbreaking and forward-thinking concepts and devices, will also pose a threat to today's "work"— and the appropriate pay that should come with it. He points to the current political framework, noting that decision makers today are not necessarily equipped to address these concerns in meaningful and mindful ways. He quotes several experts, including one who states that we are quite possibly in an age of great promise as well as great peril. Elliott is the economics editor for the Guardian.

"Fourth Industrial Revolution Brings Promise and Peril for Humanity," by Larry Elliott, January 24, 2016. Reprinted by permission.

As you read, consider the following questions:

1. Name two of the three myths of the Industrial Revolution 4.0 according to the viewpoint.
2. What did the Swiss bank UBS predict about who will benefit from this shift in the workforce toward automation?
3. What does expert Klaus Schwab say about the current climate in the workforce?

U ntil the spasm in the markets interfered, Davos 2016 was supposed to be about how humankind will cope in the new age of the smart machine. While share prices were gyrating, the bigger picture was obscured. There is a fourth industrial revolution happening and it is likely to be as profound in its effects as the previous three.

The first Industrial Revolution was about harnessing steam power so that muscle could be replaced by machines. The second was driven by electricity and a cluster of inventions from the late 19th century onwards—including the internal combustion engine, the aeroplane and moving pictures. A third revolution began in the 1960s and was based on digital technology, personal computing and the development of the internet. Industrial Revolution 4.0 will be shaped by a fresh wave of innovation in areas such as driverless cars, smart robotics, materials that are lighter and tougher, and a manufacturing process built around 3D printing.

A pity then that the World Economic Forum was overshadowed by falling share prices and the cost of oil because the impact of the fourth industrial revolution will be felt long after investors have stopped fretting about a hard landing in China.

Davos was, in some ways, a good forum for the gathering of technology pioneers, business leaders and politicians to consider some of the implications of what will be a very different sort of economy. Just to take one example, smart machines will soon be able to replace all sorts of workers, from accountants to delivery drivers and from estate agents to people handling routine motor insurance claims. On one estimate, 47% of US jobs are at risk from automation. This is Joseph Schumpeter's "gales of creative destruction" with a vengeance.

There are three myths about Industrial Revolution 4.0. The first is that it won't really have as big an impact as the previous periods of change, most especially the breakthroughs associated with the second industrial revolution. In the past, it has always taken time to feel the full effects of technological change and many of today's advances are in their infancy. It is far too early to say that the car or air travel will prove to be less important than the sequencing of the human genome or synthetic biology.

The second myth is that the process will be trouble free provided everything is left to the market. It is a fantasy to believe that the wealth created by the fourth Industrial Revolution will cascade down from rich to poor, and that those displaced will just walk into another job that pays just as well.

Indeed, all the evidence so far is that the benefits of the coming change will be concentrated among a relatively small elite, thus exacerbating the current trend towards greater levels of inequality.

This was a point stressed by the Swiss bank UBS in a report launched in Davos. It notes that there will be a "polarisation of the labour force as low-skill jobs continue to be automated and this trend increasingly spreads to middle class jobs."

A similar argument is made by Klaus Schwab, the man who runs Davos, in a book on the Fourth Industrial Revolution handed to each of the delegates at this year's World Economic Forum.

Schwab compares Detroit in 1990 with Silicon Valley in 2014. In 1990 the three biggest companies in Detroit had a market capitalisation of $36bn (£25bn), revenues of $250bn and 1.2 million employees. In 2014, the three biggest companies in Silicon Valley had a considerably higher market capitalisation ($1.09tn) generated roughly the same revenues ($247bn) but with about 10 times fewer employees (137,000).

It is easier to make money today with fewer workers than it was a quarter of a century ago. Setting up and running a car company was an expensive business and required a lot of workers. A company that makes its money out of a smart app requires less capital, doesn't have to pay for storage or transport in the way that car companies do and incurs virtually no extra costs as the number of users increases. In the jargon of economics, the marginal costs per unit of output tend towards zero and the returns to scale are high. This explains why tech entrepreneurs can get very rich very young.

Technological change has always been disruptive. There was a polarisation of income and wealth in the first wave of industrialisation at the beginning of the the 19th century, and this gave rise to political and institutional change over the 100 years between 1850 and 1950: the spread of democracy; the emergence of trade unions; progressive taxation and the development of social safety nets. These helped create bigger markets for the consumer goods that were spawned by the second Industrial Revolution: TVs, radios, vacuum cleaners and the like.

But over the past four decades a political model that both facilitated the spread of technology and provided some protection against its disruptive consequences has come under attack. Welfare states have become less generous, levels of long-term unemployment are much higher, taxation has become less progressive, politics has increasingly been dominated by those with the deepest pockets who can lobby the loudest.

Philip Jennings, general secretary of the global UNI union said: "We need some governance to ensure a democratic evolution and that requires public policy discussion. There is the opportunity to shape technology to improve people's lives; through connectivity, education, health. We shouldn't be fearful and fatalist about it."

There is, though, a third and final myth: namely that all will be well provided the fruits of an economy dominated by artificial intelligence and smart robots can be redistributed, perhaps through a citizen's income so that we can all have more leisure time when machines do all the work.

But redistribution, even assuming it happens, is only part of the story. Making his first visit to Davos, the Archbishop of Canterbury said the changes likely to be brought about required not just an economic but also a spiritual response. "This is not just about money, it is about what it is to be human", said Justin Welby.

Schwab said: "The changes are so profound that, from the perspective of human history, there has never been a time of greater promise or potential peril. My concern, however, is that decision makers are too often caught in traditional, linear (and non-disruptive) thinking or too absorbed by immediate concerns to think strategically about the forces of disruption and innovation shaping our future."

He's right, although there is a simpler way of putting it: faced with the challenge of disruptive new technology, the current political framework is no longer fit for purpose and its shortcomings are likely to lead to a backlash that could turn very nasty. That should concern not just Schwab and the Archbishop of Canterbury but also the investment bankers of Wall Street and the tech billionaires of Silicon Valley.

> *"Without needing to own our own vehicles anymore, we'd save on gas, maintenance, parking, and insurance costs."*

The Benefits of Self-Driving Cars Will Outweigh the Drawbacks, Including Job Loss

Joel Lee

In the following viewpoint, Joel Lee argues that while the full implementation of automation such as self-driving cars would undoubtedly lead to losses in many areas of employment, the advantages would still make the transition worthwhile. On the losses side, direct impact would be the loss of work for truck drivers, Uber (and other ride-sharing service) drivers, and bus drivers, in addition to repair shop employees. On the positive side, crash rates would see a drastic decrease, as would cargo losses (as accident rates would go down). Cost savings on insurance, gas, and the time spent in traffic and parking would, for many, be life altering. Lee is the editor in chief of MakeUseOf.

"Self Driving Cars Endanger Millions of American Jobs (And That's Okay)," by Joel Lee, Makeuseof, June 19, 2015. Reprinted by permission.

As you read, consider the following questions:

1. Name three of the types of jobs that would be lost if driverless cars became the norm.
2. What company's self-driving vehicles saw only 11 accidents in six years of test drives?
3. How would the "one car per person" concept change, in an age of driverless cars?

The self-driving car is technology's biggest gift to civilization since the birth of the Internet. It'll be a few decades before driverless cars become the norm, but when that day comes, it will be glorious. Robot cars will restore mobility to the young, elderly, and disabled. They'll make travel cheaper and safer. In short, they're going to change the world.

This impending revolution comes with one huge drawback: robot cars are going to destroy a lot of jobs.

With companies like Tesla already pushing for autonomous features as early as this coming summer, the threat against American jobs is immediate. But just how many jobs will be lost? And is this economic loss justified? The answers may surprise you.

Which Jobs Are at Risk, Exactly?

Not long ago, the first self-driving truck was released into the wild. Freightliner's Inspiration, with its ceremonial license plate of AU 010, is the biggest milestone to be hit since the autonomous vehicle discussion began. It's only legal in Nevada at the moment, and it has a human driver as backup, but it's a monumental step just the same.

According to the Bureau of Labor Statistics, there were approximately 1.6 million American truck drivers in 2014 earning a mean income of $42,000. That's more than half a percent of the country, and $67 billion dollars in income—about 0.3% of the US GDP.

These new trucks aren't completely autonomous yet, but the technology is going to get there sooner rather than later. And when that day arrives, those truck drivers will need to find something else to do. When you include delivery truck operators, which numbered around 800,000 in 2014, we end up with 2.4 million people who may be out of a job in the next decade or two.

But the bigger topic of conversation when it comes to self-driving cars and their impact? Service drivers. Mainly we're talking about taxi drivers—and more recently, Uber drivers—but also included in the conversation are people like bus drivers.

As autonomous vehicle technology improves, it's easy to imagine a world where these vehicles have no need for a human operator. This would leave the following people jobless: 180,000 taxi drivers, 160,000 Uber drivers, 500,000 school bus drivers, and 160,000 transit bus drivers, for a grand total of 1 million jobs.

And if we extrapolate a bit and throw in a dash of speculation, we can look at the potential impact on peripheral jobs that don't involve direct driving but do provide services to modern day consumer drivers. For example, auto body repair shops.

While driverless cars are nowhere near perfect in terms of safety, they are undoubtedly safer than the average American driver. Over 6 years of public testing, Google's vehicles have only been in 11 minor accidents, and if Google's reports are trustworthy, none of those accidents were caused by the autonomous vehicle.

A study by McKinsey & Company predicts that, in a future where all cars are driverless, we could see a crash rate reduction of up to 90 percent. Lower accident rates would lead to less frequent visits to auto body repair shops, and that would leave a good portion of the 445,000 auto body repairers without a job.

Other peripherally-impacted jobs could include street meter maids, parking lot attendants, gas station attendants, rental car agencies, and more. Not all of these would lose their jobs entirely, but it's hard to imagine that these industries wouldn't be drastically affected, which could affect up to 220,000 more workers.

In total, that's a little over 4 million American jobs put at risk due to the coming revolution in self-driving cars—more than 1% of the country. Do note that this change will tend result in reemployment rather than unemployment, leading to an overall boost in economic productivity, provided the economy continues to expand.

The Economic Benefits of Self-Driving Cars

Now that we've determined how many potential jobs are at risk, let's look at the potential benefits that we can enjoy once autonomous cars become the norm. Will these benefits justify those lost jobs? I'll illustrate what we stand to gain, but only you can decide whether the trade will be worth it.

As mentioned earlier, the McKinsey prediction is that a society of self-driving cars could see a reduction in crash rates up to 90 percent. For the individual, this means less money spent on car repairs, maintenance, and health bills related to automotive accidents—which is estimated to be around $180 billion per year.

On a wider scale, we get fewer accidents when transporting cargo over long distances, so companies save money on lost goods. There's also a slight safety increase since fuel tankers and other volatile vehicles are less prone to crash and burn, but admittedly the gains here may not be significant.

Going back to individual benefits, many regions might move away from the "one car per person" mentality that we currently possess, especially in urban environments. Imagine this: whenever you need a car, you open an app and request one, and it's there in a few minutes. Uber is already faster than an ambulance in cities like London. Robot cars can probably get that number smaller. When you get to your destination, there's no need to find parking —the car simply drives away.

Without needing to own our own vehicles anymore, we'd save on gas, maintenance, parking, and insurance costs.

More remarkably, imagine a scenario in which all of these cars were hooked into a singular network. In essence, cars would talk to one another wirelessly as they traveled, and this kind of hivemind would be a huge step towards more efficient driving. People going to the same places could be pooled, sending buses along popular routes, and smart-cars for one-off trips. Electric cars could be used more easily, since they could charge themselves without needing to inconvenience a person. All of this amounts to huge savings. Using autonomous vehicles could wind up costing only a few cents per mile.

A practical example of this kind of hivemind network would be the case of inner city parking. In places like New York, it's almost impossible to find parking because we all want to park as close to our destination as possible. With autonomous cars, that's no longer necessary. The car can immediately go help someone else when you're done with it. No more waiting around depreciating and using up space. How many hours of your life have been wasted in search of a place to park? Now you can arrive at your destination, step out, and go on with your day—the car will do the same.

Another practical example of the automotive hivemind: traffic efficiency. Did you know that your vehicle's fuel economy rating is based on optimal conditions? If you aren't driving like a perfect robot, you aren't getting anywhere near the fuel economy that you think you are.

For example, the most fuel-efficient way to drive is the "pulse and glide method," which involves a rhythmic alternating between acceleration and coasting. Anything less than that and you're wasting gas. Gas-powered autonomous cars can be programmed with optimal driving behavior, which saves on gas.

But more importantly, optimal driving behavior leads to minimal congestion. Did you know that many traffic jams occur simply due to human inefficiency?

A study by INRIX found that the average American and European driver wastes about 111 hours in gridlock every year.

What would you do with an extra 111 hours? With driverless cars, gridlock could be a thing of the past.

What else could we get by cutting humans out of the driving equation?

Perhaps the biggest benefit of the driverless car is that they don't suffer from human flaws. Machines have no need to sleep, which means around-the-clock operation of vehicles, but it also means that they aren't burdened by drowsiness. That's an additional point for the "autonomous cars are safer" column.

Another cost that passes down to the customer: insurance premiums. Insurance rates are calculated based on risk. Since we've already established that driverless cars are significantly safer than the average human driver, insurance costs will plummet. Plus, most of those costs will shift to manufacturers and operators of said cars, leaving us free of that burden.

There are so many more benefits to explore, but I'll end with one that's particularly poignant in light of Tesla's recent advancements in battery technology: the fact that driverless cars are more friendly for the environment.

Most of the aforementioned benefits are about cost savings and gas efficiency: less gridlock, less idling, less searching for parking, and more use of electric vehicles? If we follow that thread, the natural conclusion is that improved efficiency leads to reduced carbon emissions. That's always a good thing.

There are other factors to consider, which you can read about in our defense that autonomous cars are good for the environment.

A New Era Is Around the Corner

The truth is that the advent of a driverless car industry will surely displace more jobs than it will create, but the long-term gains that we'll see as a society far outweigh the short-term growing pains and inconveniences. The economic, environmental, and human benefits are astounding. I truly believe that this is one of the situations where the loss of jobs is a valid sacrifice for the greater good of society.

Would I be singing the same tune if self-writing robots were also on the horizon, threatening my own job? If they offered the same kind of economic value and social benefits as self-driving cars, you bet. Self-driving cars are simply too good to pass up.

"You now have got robots that can see in three-dimension and that's getting much better and also becoming much less expensive."

Automation Poses a Threat to White-Collar Jobs, Too

National Public Radio

In the following viewpoint, National Public Radio (NPR) argues that while repetitive jobs, particularly in manufacturing, have seen the effects of automation, jobs driven by less clear-cut tasks, such as those requiring more visual perception and dexterity, as well as decision making, are also at risk as robots and computer software become more advanced. This includes the food preparation field as well as reporting jobs. NPR is a national news organization in the U.S. whose mission is "to work in partnership with Member Stations to create a more informed public—one challenged and invigorated by a deeper understanding and appreciation of events, ideas and cultures."

"Attention White-Collar Workers: The Robots Are Coming For Your Jobs," Fresh Air with Terry Gross is produced by WHYY in Philadelphia and distributed by NPR, May 18, 2015. Reprinted by permission.

As you read, consider the following questions:

1. What kinds of jobs have we come to expect to be replaced by robots and software?
2. What limitations have robots and automated jobs had in the past that are no longer as much of a concern?
3. What are some of the creative jobs robots and computers are moving toward in the present day?

F rom the self-checkout aisle of the grocery store to the sports section of the newspaper, robots and computer software are increasingly taking the place of humans in the workforce. Silicon Valley executive Martin Ford says that robots, once thought of as a threat to only manufacturing jobs, are poised to replace humans as teachers, journalists, lawyers and others in the service sector.

"There's already a hardware store [in California] that has a customer service robot that, for example, is capable of leading customers to the proper place on the shelves in order to find an item," Ford tells *Fresh Air*'s Dave Davies.

In his new book, *Rise of the Robots*, Ford considers the social and economic disruption that is likely to result when educated workers can no longer find employment.

"As we look forward from this point, we need to keep in mind that this technology is going to continue to accelerate," Ford says. "So I think there's every reason to believe it's going to become the primary driver of inequality in the future, and things are likely to get even more extreme than they are now."

Interview Highlights
On Robots in Manufacturing
Any jobs that are truly repetitive or rote—doing the same thing again and again—in advanced economies like the United States or Germany, those jobs are long gone. They've already been replaced by robots years and years ago.

So what we've seen in manufacturing is that the jobs that are actually left for people to do tend to be the ones that require more flexibility or require visual perception and dexterity. Very often these jobs kind of fill in the gaps between machines. For example, feeding parts into the next part of the production process or very often they're at the end of the process—perhaps loading and unloading trucks and moving raw materials and finished products around, those types of things.

But what we're seeing now in robotics is that finally the machines are coming for those jobs as well, and this is being driven by advances in areas like visual perception. You now have got robots that can see in three-dimension and that's getting much better and also becoming much less expensive. So you're beginning to see machines that are starting to have the kind of perception and dexterity that begins to approach what human beings can do. A lot more jobs are becoming susceptible to this and that's something that's going to continue to accelerate, and more and more of those jobs are going to disappear and factories are just going to relentlessly approach full-automation where there really aren't going to be many people at all.

On the New Generation of Robot Jobs

There's a company here in Silicon Valley called Industrial Perception which is focused specifically on loading and unloading boxes and moving boxes around. This is a job that up until recently would've been beyond the robots because it relies on visual perception often in varied environments where the lighting may not be perfect and so forth, and where the boxes may be stacked haphazardly instead of precisely and it has been very, very difficult for a robot to take that on. But they've actually built a robot that's very sophisticated and may eventually be able to move boxes about one per second and that would compare with about one per every six seconds for a particularly efficient person. So it's dramatically faster and, of course, a robot that moves boxes is never going to get tired.

It's never going to get injured. It's never going to file a workers' compensation claim.

On a Robot That's Being Built for Use in the Fast Food Industry

Essentially, it's a machine that produces very, very high quality hamburgers. It can produce about 350 to 400 per hour; they come out fully configured on a conveyor belt ready to serve to the customer. ... It's all fresh vegetables and freshly ground meat and so forth; it's not frozen patties like you might find at a fast food joint. These are actually much higher quality hamburgers than you'd find at a typical fast food restaurant. ... They're building a machine that's actually quite compact that could potentially be used not just in fast food restaurants but in convenience stores and also maybe in vending machines.

On Automated Farming

In Japan they've got a robot that they use now to pick strawberries and it can do that one strawberry every few seconds and it actually operates at night so that they can operate around the clock picking strawberries. What we see in agriculture is that's the sector that has already been the most dramatically impacted by technology and, of course, mechanical technologies—it was tractors and harvesters and so forth. There are some areas of agriculture now that are almost essentially, you could say, fully automated.

On Computer-written News Stories

Essentially it looks at the raw data that's provided from some source, in this case from the baseball game, and it translates that into a real narrative. It's quite sophisticated. It doesn't simply take numbers and fill in the blanks in a formulaic report. It has the ability to actually analyze the data and figure out what things are important, what things are most interesting, and then it can actually weave that into a very compelling narrative. ... They're generating thousands and thousands of stories. In fact, the number I heard was about one story every 30 seconds is being generated automatically and that they appear on a number of websites and in the news media. Forbes is one that we know about. Many of the others that use this particular service aren't eager to disclose that. ... Right now it tends to be focused on those areas that you might consider to be a bit more formulaic, for example sports reporting and also financial reporting—things like earnings reports for companies and so forth.

On Computers Starting to Do Creative Work

Right now it's the more routine formulaic jobs—jobs that are predictable, the kinds of jobs where you tend to do the same kinds of things again and again—those jobs are really being heavily impacted. But it's important to realize that that could change in the future. We already see a number of areas, like [a] program that was able to produce [a] symphony, where computers are beginning to exhibit creativity—they can actually create new things from scratch. ... [There is] a painting program which actually can generate original art; not to take a photograph and Photoshop it or something, but to actually generate original art.

Periodical and Internet Sources Bibliography

The following articles have been selected to supplement the diverse views presented in this chapter.

Jamie Bartlett, "Will 2018 Be the Year of the Neo-Luddite?," *Guardian*, March 4, 2018. theguardian.com/technology/2018/mar/04/will -2018-be-the-year-of-the-neo-luddite.

James Bessen, "The Automation Paradox," Atlantic.com, January 19, 2016. theatlantic.com/business/archive/2016/01/automation -paradox/424437.

Joe Carmichael, "Will Modern Luddites Attack Robots as the Automation Revolution Takes Hold?," Inverse.com, May 19, 2016. inverse.com/article/15773-will-modern-luddites-attack-robots -as-the-automation-revolution-takes-hold.

James Doubek, "Automation Could Displace 800 Million Workers Worldwide by 2030," NPR, November 30, 2017. npr.org/sections /alltechconsidered/2017/11/30/567408644/automation-could -displace-800-million-workers-worldwide-by-2030-study-says.

June Javelosa and Kristin Houser, "This Company Replaced 90% of Its Workforce with Machines. Here's What Happened," weforum.org, February 16, 2017. weforum.org/agenda/2017/02/after -replacing-90-of-employees-with-robots-this-companys -productivity-soared.

Vinnie Merchandani, "Forget Luddite Workers. Luddite customers are bigger roadblocks to automation," *Enterprise Irregulars*, November 18, 2016. enterpriseirregulars.com/111521 /forget-luddite-workers-luddite-customers-bigger-roadblocks -automation.

Tejvan Pettinger, "The Luddite Fallacy," EconomicsHelp.org, January 15, 2017. economicshelp.org/blog/6717/economics/the -luddite-fallacy.

Clive Thompson, "When Robots Take All of Our Jobs, Remember the Luddites," Smithsonian.com, January 2017. smithsonianmag .com/innovation/when-robots-take-jobs-remember -luddites-180961423.

Unknown, "Automation and the Workforce: What's the Real
Challenge?," robotics.org, April 25, 2017. robotics.org/blog
-article.cfm/Automation-and-the-Workforce-What-s-the-Real
-Challenge/38.

Unknown, "The Luddite Fallacy: How AI Will Change the Jobs We
Do," blogs.opentext.com, May 11, 2017. blogs.opentext.com
/luddite-fallacy-ai-will-change-jobs.

OPPOSING
VIEWPOINTS®
SERIES

CHAPTER 3

Will the Automation of Labor Generate Any New Growth?

Chapter Preface

B esides convenience, what are the benefits to automated labor? Are they enough to offset disruptions to the workforce and marked economic shifts that developed countries are likely to experience? Will the automation of labor generate growth in the job market?

The gig economy (think Uber, AirBNB, TaskRabbit) and service opportunities like restaurants and health and wellness are growing as automated labor rates increase. However, as the gig economy grows, the security of steady employment—and the benefits that usually accompany it—decreases.

Education, particularly personalized learning, is also worth examining in this context. Teachers and professors may be getting shut out of job opportunities if fewer instructors are needed, as students can register for large online courses. The upside, however, is that job prospects may increase for students who now have access to education opportunities that were not previously available to them. When this happens, though, is the education these students are receiving of equal value and strength to more personalized education?

The viewpoints in this chapter explore job sectors with predicted growth. One supports the idea that as some markets shrink, they may be replaced with better positions, with the right training. This can pave the way to true career mobility for people who have been replaced by automation in their original or previous roles. Another supports the idea that automation is ultimately a job creator, with a nod to productivity gains and limits to automation.

Another viewpoint argues that there will forever be a need for teachers, even as their roles and responsibilities shift with innovations and advances in technology. Yet another, on the other hand, isn't as "sold" on the true impact of personalized learning now, and what it will be in the future. In their viewpoint, they consider the role of technology in personalized learning and look at how teachers can fit into that.

The merits of personalized learning are also discussed. Some believe that this approach is a better way for students to really hone their skills in the "Four Cs:" communication, collaboration, critical thinking, and creativity.

| "*It's important to do research on the job market, look at salary trends by geographic location, and think about possibilities for growth over time in specific roles.*"

It Is Possible to Retrain Post Automation

Erin Carson

In the following viewpoint, Erin Carson argues that automation is not necessarily the road to unemployment and that people who are replaced by automation can often be retrained into new—and sometimes better—positions. The author points out many ways the tech industry remains a viable possibility for career mobility. With this in mind, it is critical that anyone at risk of losing a job to automation take appropriate steps to broaden their skill set and become an expert in their field. Carson is a staff reporter at CNET.

As you read, consider the following questions:

1. How does Oxford economist Carl Benedikt Frey say we have always adapted?
2. According to the TPR survey cited in the viewpoint, which areas of tech are most likely to become automated?
3. How does the Baxter robot learn to do its job?

R obots—they're the economic threat du jour.
In the past several years, we've seen a variety of numbers describing just how unemployed the human race will be when automation creeps through the workforce like a bad frost.

But, we're not there yet.

Whether the robots are going to put us all out of work is not a yes or no situation. Loosely, the lay of the land is something like this: Some people will lose jobs. Some people will retrain, or be retrained by their company. Some will work in jobs that did not exist before automation.

So, what to do? If anything at all?

The lesson to glean might just be the importance of a strong and always-expanding skillset.

"It's definitely true that we have always adapted by acquiring new skills that are complementary to the arrival of new technologies," said Oxford economist Carl Benedikt Frey.

Frey, as well as Michael Osborne of the Oxford Martin School co-authored the oft-cited 2013 study called, The Future of Employment: How susceptible are jobs to computerisation? The study concluded that 47% of US employment is at risk of computerization over the course of an unspecified amount of time.

Featured is a graph that shows the jobs least likely to be automated are in management, business and financial, and computers, engineering, and science.

Frey told ZDNet that while there's debate as to whether automation will most heavily affect low skills jobs, or also affect knowledge work, generally they found that those with more education, with PhDs or professional degrees particularly in STEM fields, are least susceptible to computerization.

It's impossible to write a prescription for the retraining needs of such a wide swath of jobs, but this might be yet another incentive to turn to tech.

"Students and those seeking to switch industries, whether for fear of automation or otherwise, should certainly look into technology. The tech industry continues to create plentiful opportunities for job seekers in a variety of sectors and roles, which would be a valuable career choice for anyone in the job market," Robert Half's senior executive director John Reed said.

For those already working in the technology industry, Tech Pro Research recently conducted a survey called The Future of IT Jobs: How to Beat the Machines. Already some indicators are emerging as to what people are experiencing and expecting as far as automation in their jobs.

Thirty-six percent of respondents said that "automation caused people to be moved into equal or higher-level positions." Fifty-six percent said they have training programs to help employees advance their knowledge in response to automation, and 78 percent of those programs are done in-house. Another 62 percent of respondents are using self-study to keep up their skills in response to automation.

As hinted at, retraining can take all sorts of forms.

For those not already working in tech, Reed advised this: "A fondness for technology and the willingness to keep up in an environment that is constantly changing is certainly a key factor [that] anyone looking to make the move into technology should consider."

It's important to do research on the job market, look at salary trends by geographic location, and think about possibilities for growth over time in specific roles.

"Just like any career—you want to ensure that once you've invested in training, you'll have a career path that offers advancement," Reed said.

And that's important, because some areas are healthier than others.

The TPR survey also found that the three departments most likely to experience automation are system administration, data center, and help desk. Also, those departments are the top three reporting the loss of jobs as a result of automation.

Retraining to stay in tech could be somewhat easier. Those in "at risk" jobs might consider getting a jump on expanding their skillset before something dramatic happens. Best case: a smoother transition. Worst case: a new set of marketable skills at ready access.

Though, Frey said, just because people become educated, doesn't necessarily mean new jobs are being created for them to fill.

Some of this burden falls on companies and their hiring policies, he said.

"You need to invest, you need to create new opportunities, and I think such investments will need to accommodate education to create new future jobs for people coming up in the labor market to be employed," Frey said.

Though, it is worth noting the recent push from the White House projects there will be 1 million open jobs in information technology by 2020.

So if that's a desirable route, it's a matter of deciding on a type of tech job and picking a course of action that could include online courses, coding camps, or other accelerated technology programs, Reed said.

As far as retraining within a company, J.P. Gownder, vice president and principal analyst with Forrester Research, gave an example of Rethink Robotics' Baxter robot. It's an assembly line robot, but instead of being programmed by computer scientists, the workers who were doing the manual task take the robot's arm and perform that task in order to train the robot.

Gownder talked about the idea of job transformation.

"Robots aren't so much stealing our jobs as they are becoming a part of our work environment," he said, "and so no matter what your skill level is, there may be opportunities for you to retrain into something that works with the robots rather than being replaced by the robots."

That's been the case at business processing and tech firm Xchanging. They introduced robotic process automation (RPA) in 2014. As an outsourcing provider, they were looking to find ways to be more innovative, said Paul Donaldson, Xchanging's head of robotics.

"The nature of the game for BPOs [business process outsourcing] is to try and continually innovate and find more benefits for our customer base, financial benefits or improvements in turnaround time or quality, or all these kinds of niches," he said.

They started off in their insurance offering, processing work for Lloyd's (the global specialty insurance market in London).

In short, Xchanging has taken a lot of work that folks weren't keen on doing anyway (like closing static insurance claims), moved some of those people into more client-facing roles, and some of them into roles actually dealing with the RPAs, and despite the fact they've got 27 robots running, no one's lost their job.

Instead, they're learning to work with these bits of software—they've even named them. One RPA went live around Remembrance Day, so they named it Poppy, and now even Donaldson realizes he refers to Poppy like a person.

Another possibility is that automation could create jobs that didn't exist before. Gownder gave an example of the parking garage at the airport in Dusseldorf, Germany. They introduced a robot valet, basically, that parks cars by lifting them up and putting them into spots. Post automation, the garage can accommodate about 40% more cars. And while previously there was no one working in that garage, there now has to be a trained technician on staff to maintain, repair, and oversee the system.

Going back to the Xchanging example, Donaldson's job is one that wouldn't exist without the move to automation. Similarly, each robot has a handler of sorts who organizes the robot's workload, as well as trains it for any new tasks.

"If you looked at the next 10 years, the likelihood is that yes, there will be some job losses, but there will also be opportunities," Gownder said.

"One industry may disappear, but another more specialized occupation might rise in its place."

Automation Allows Humans to Do Other—More Significant—Work

Quartz Media

In the following viewpoint, Quartz Media argues that automation is a job creator and that the jobs that come as a result of automation are often better opportunities than the ones whose demise came about as a result of automation. In addition, the potential for productivity gains needs to be taken into account. Conversely, however, the article notes that automation is limited by Polanyi's paradox—the idea that we can't necessarily describe things we are particularly good at, particularly in the fine arts, for example. Quartz Media is a content outlet that covers the global economy. The organization has journalists around the world, writing for a range of platforms.

"Robots Won't Take Your Job—They'll Help Make Room for Meaningful Work Instead," Quartz Media LLC, March 15, 2017. Reprinted by permission.

As you read, consider the following questions:

1. Which president delivered a final address that included the note, "The next wave of economic dislocations won't come from overseas. It will come from the relentless pace of automation that makes a lot of good, middle-class jobs obsolete"?
2. Describe the ATM example provided in the article— what happened to the population of bank tellers after the increase in ATMs around the United States?
3. What is the idea explained by the concept called Polanyi's paradox?

Unencumbered by the prospect of re-election, outgoing presidents tend to use their final speeches to candidly warn against threats they believe to be metastasizing in society. For example, George Washington spoke of the ills of hyper-partisanship and excessive debt. Dwight Eisenhower denounced the waxing power of the "military industrial complex." President Barack Obama singled out an economic peril in his otherwise doggedly hopeful final address in Chicago: "The next wave of economic dislocations won't come from overseas," he said. "It will come from the relentless pace of automation that makes a lot of good, middle-class jobs obsolete."

Obama articulated a fear felt by many around the world: That all our jobs will eventually be done by robots. Research backs this fear: One study found that automation will threaten at least 47% of jobs in America and up to 85% in the rest of the world. But a number of economists are beginning to argue that this view of automation excludes a lot of the story.

Putting Automation in Context

To simply argue that automation is going to gobble up jobs ignores the potential for productivity gains. The Business Harvard Review found that the IT revolution led to 0.6% labor productivity growth and 1% of overall growth in Europe, the US, and Japan between 1995 and 2005. "It all hinges on demand," says Jim Bessen, professor of economics at Boston University. If the productivity gains are enough to significantly boost demand, then job growth may be the result. This is especially true when new technologies create jobs that simply did not exist before, such as social-media managers. In those cases, any jobs created will make a net contribution to the labor market.

Though automation will cost some jobs, it will also create many others. A case in point is the rollout of ATMs in the US. Introduced in the 1970s, the number of ATMs increased from 100,000 to 400,000 between 1995 and 2010. Running an ATM is cheaper than paying a teller's salary, so as ATMs became more numerous relative to tellers, the overall cost of each bank branch came down. As it became cheaper to operate a bank branch, more of them opened, ultimately resulting in the number of bank branches increasing by 40% between 1988 and 2004. This means that more tellers were hired to staff these branches, not less. Instead of ATMs putting bank tellers out of work, US bank-teller employment actually increased over the three decades between 1980 and 2010. The reason for the growth was the added productivity gains brought on by automation.

The textile industry is another example of this phenomenon. Despite the fact that 98% of the functions of making materials have now been automated, the number of weaving jobs has increased since the 19th century. As with the ATM example, automation drove the price of cloth down, which increased demand—and eventually caused more job growth.

There is also evidence to suggest that automation can lead to the substitution of one occupation for another. In other words: It's true that typesetters may no longer be in demand—but graphic designers are. One industry may disappear, but another more specialized occupation might rise in its place. What's more, jobs that include a high level of automation, like software development and accounting, are growing faster than other jobs in the economy.

The Opportunities of Partial Automation

A lot of the debate around automation ignores the fact that most of it is partial—that not all of the work is taken over by machines. In fact, only one of the 270 occupations listed in the 1950 census has been eliminated thanks to automation: elevator operators.

This is an important distinction. If a job is completely automated, then jobs will indeed ultimately be eliminated. But if the process is only partial, employment for that job may in fact increase because of the efficiency gains and possible effects on demand. It's also worth noting that fewer than 5% of jobs in the US could be completely automated using current technology.

David Autor, professor of economics at MIT, adds that the remaining non-automated tasks "tend to become more valuable." This is because automation is likely to take over mundane or repetitive tasks, leaving professionals more time to do the things that really require their skills. For instance, automation will help mortgage-loan officers spend less time scouring paperwork when processing loan applications and free them up to issue more mortgages. Similarly, in the sphere of health care, if the diagnosis of most conditions can be automated, emergency rooms could combine triage and diagnosis, letting doctors focus on special cases, increasing the number of patients being treated overall.

This trend is even true in the era of artificial intelligence (AI). In the legal sphere, a bot's ability to sift through large volumes of legal documents using software during the "discovery" phase of a trial was thought to reduce the number of the legal clerks and paralegals who traditionally performed this role. Instead, by reducing the cost of discovery, automation increased demand for it. The number of paralegals has increased since the introduction of discovery software in 1990.

The Limits to Automation

At the moment, automation does not appear to be infinite. It is constrained by what economists call Polanyi's paradox. Named after Karl Polanyi, who in 1966 observed "We know more than

Self-Education Can Prove Valuable in the Age of Automation

The challenge we face as educators to prepare our students for uncertain futures and an ever-changing workforce isn't anything new. That's a big reason the district vision was reshaped years ago to put key 21st century capacities at the center of recent curriculum revisions. Multiple studies have shown that large numbers of jobs are at risk as programmed devices and automated systems continue to seep into the workplace. With workplace automation on the rise, the question of how we educate people for an automated world becomes even more pressing.

A recent *New York Times* article "How to Prepare for an Automated Future" is a great read that affirms much of what we're currently doing in our classrooms. The article touches on all of our 21st Century Capacities, making the claim that schools will need to teach the traits and skills that machines cannot easily reproduce—creativity, critical thinking, emotional intelligence, self-direction, and collaboration.

This quote reminded me of a conversation I had recently with a good friend who does not work in education, but as a marketing and communications director. He was explaining to me how more than ever his job demands adaptability and new learning. As industries constantly evolve and the foundations of our economy remain somewhat shaky, he can't rely on the stability of one or two jobs that span his entire career. In the ten years that I've known him, he's had successful jobs for three different architecture firms and, as of two weeks ago, a construction company. As he splits his time between an architecture firm and the construction company, he must now, on his own, "up-skill" by teaching himself key aspects of the construction industry. This means knowing which questions to ask and involves a great deal of online research. In short, it means knowing how to learn.

Is my friend complaining? Not at all. And it's because he's positioned himself to work in a field that cannot be easily automated or outsourced, and he's honed his skills and his capacity to learn (often leveraging technology) in a way that allows him be more efficient with his time and resources. This increased efficiency has expanded his opportunities for more work and income, yet not at the expense of time away from his family and personal interests.

"Teaching for an Automated Future," by Michael Kiefer, Learning Personalized.

we can tell," the paradox refers to the difficulty in automating an activity that we only understand tacitly: Painting a picture, writing a persuasive argument, or dancing are all tasks that even people who are highly proficient in them are not fully able to describe. We cannot program what we cannot understand. True, there is evidence that machine learning capable of "understanding" such tasks tacitly might eliminate this hurdle, but for the time being, professions that require flexibility and creativity are quite resistant to obsolescence.

In the short to medium term, the main effect of automation will not necessarily be eliminating jobs, but redefining them. As the skills and tasks required in the economy change, our response should not be alarmism or protectionism, but a strategic investment in education—which was, incidentally, one of the last policies Obama pushed for in office.

"One thing that is going to change, however, is the need for teachers with technological skills."

Computers Will Not Replace Teachers

Sarah Marsh

In the following viewpoint, Sarah Marsh argues that, while technology is playing an increasingly prominent role in education, teachers are still needed and should not feel threatened by it. While some programs utilize computers to supplement and even replace teachers, the need for trained educators remains relevant. And while a "dramatic shift" in teaching may be on the horizon, their importance continues to be recognized. However, Marsh points out, in no uncertain terms, that teachers with a strong handle on technology will fare far better in the coming iterations of education. Marsh is a news reporter at the Guardian.

As you read, consider the following questions:

1. What are some of the ways computers are being used in classrooms today?
2. What is blended learning?
3. What are two ways teaching will likely change in the coming years, with regard to increased use of computers?

In the early 1960s work was underway in a US laboratory on a project that had the potential to revolutionise education. Professor Donald Bitzer, an electrical engineer at the University of Illinois, was creating one of the world's first teaching machines. By 1972 his software had gone from serving a single classroom to being used across America.

But with its growth came speculation and apprehension—could a computer replace a teacher?

"Computers at this time were viewed as gigantic brains that would control our lives," says historian Brian Dear. Bitzer's software—known as the Programmed Logic for Automated Teaching Operations (PLATO)—let students answer questions on six-inch black screens using teletype keyboards costing around £5,000 a terminal.

Forty years on, the question of whether computers could render teachers obsolete is still being asked. Fiona Hollands, senior researcher at Columbia University's Teachers College, says computers are now being used for several distinct reasons in the classroom: they help face-to-face teacher instruction in "blended learning" models; can be used to supplement educators in "hybrid" teaching models; and replace teachers in "virtual" classrooms.

"A few states and districts have created their own virtual schools with Florida Virtual School being the best known," says Hollands, adding that a recent study claimed not only can students do just as well with this approach, but there may also be cost savings.

In the US, Rocketship schools have cut overheads by introducing more online classes and employing fewer teachers. They have attracted global attention through their "blended learning" approach in which a quarter of a student's school day is taught by a computer. Teachers without credentials supervise online sessions while qualified teachers focus on critical thinking. Any savings are used to pay existing teachers more.

Speaking on British radio in 2014, the chief executive of Rocketship, Preston Smith, said that computers had let them "re-think" the school day. But Gordon Lafer, a political economist and University of Oregon professor, thinks they offer a "stripped down program of study."

Hollands argued that Rocketship schools provide a lower quality education to deprived children. He believes it is hard, for example, to work alone online if your English reading skills are weak and if you are easily distracted.

The UK version of Rocketship, Ark Pioneer academy, will open its doors next year. But Christine Blower, general secretary of the National Union of Teachers, has been sceptical. Speaking to the Daily Mail last year, she said that if children end up sitting in front of computers for a significant amount of time, with no routine access to a teacher for every lesson, then that would be a "wrong departure."

Tricia Kelleher, principal of the Stephen Perse Foundation, warns that technology should not spell the end for teachers. Rather, it should be seen as a useful tool in the teacher's armoury. "If you're no longer just standing up and delivering instruction you need to think how that changes the way you teach," she says.

Sugata Mitra, professor of educational technology at the School of Education, Communication and Language Sciences at Newcastle University, thinks that in the future the role of teachers will be similar to that of a football coach. "Children can now go out into cyberspace and the teacher is the friend at the back telling them where they might need to go," he says.

In May 2013, Mitra did a Ted talk on the "school in the cloud" where he discussed his hole in the wall experiment. Mitra placed a computer in a kiosk in a Delhi slum and allowed children to use it freely. He found that many of them, lots who had never seen a computer, could teach themselves all on their own.

"Teachers often ask me, am I going to lose my job? I say no because your job will get harder. It will become a different job. It will go from being a master standing at the front of class to a helpful friend at the back." He adds: "There will have to be a dramatic change to teacher programmes but we are no where near that yet."

One thing that is going to change, however, is the need for teachers with technological skills. José Picardo, the assistant principal of Surbiton High school, says teachers who can use technology will replace those who cannot. He adds that tools like video now allow children to learn at any point, and teachers need to make the most of this.

But in this complex debate there's one thing that continues to reassure Plato developer David Woolley: "Will computers replace a teacher? It never came to pass then and I doubt it ever will. Humans are social animals and there is something about the human connection between students and teachers that matters a lot. That is not to say that other means of teaching are not valuable. They are, but there are things that a computer will never be able to do as a good human teacher."

*"Personalized Learning appears
to be promising for improving
student achievement."*

Personalized Learning Is Likely Effective in the Short Term

John F. Pane, Elizabeth D. Steiner, Matthew D. Baird, Laura S. Hamilton, and Joseph D. Pane

In the following viewpoint, John F. Pane, Elizabeth D. Steiner, Matthew D. Baird, Laura S. Hamilton, and Joseph D. Pane argue that the long-term impact of personalized learning is unclear but that on a short-term basis it can improve achievement. They compare the approach to more typical teaching practices and also factor in the ways in which technology plays a role in this approach and how teachers can be part of its implementation. The authors all work for the RAND Corporation: John F. Pane is a senior scientist; Steiner is an associate policy researcher; Baird is co-director of the Center for Causal Inference; Hamilton is a senior behavioral scientist; and Joseph D. Pane is a statistical analyst.

Pane, John F., Elizabeth D. Steiner, Matthew D. Baird, Laura S. Hamilton and Joseph D. Pane, "How Does Personalized Learning Affect Student Achievement?" Santa Monica, CA: RAND Corporation, RB-9994-BMGF, 2017. As of October 8, 2018: rand.org/pubs /research_briefs/RB9994.html.

As you read, consider the following questions:

1. Describe the working definition of Personalized Learning.
2. How did charter schools do in comparison to districts, in terms of achievement?
3. Over how long was this initial analysis completed?

Interest in schoolwide personalized learning (PL) models is growing across the nation. While PL and its focus on individualized instruction seems to be a promising concept, a critical question remains: Does PL improve student learning more than other educational approaches? RAND Education experts partnered with the Bill and Melinda Gates Foundation to begin to answer this question.

Personalized learning (PL) refers to practices that tailor the pace and focus of instruction to address the needs and goals of each student. In recent years, schools and school districts have begun to adopt schoolwide PL models. Because the PL approach is sensitive to student interests and areas of academic strength or weakness, the programs have the potential to increase student learning and engagement.

While PL is promising in theory, there are very few evaluations of students' learning outcomes in such programs. The research described in this brief begins to fill this gap by presenting an evaluation of PL schools and student achievement based on fall 2014 and spring 2015 mathematics and reading test scores. The schools received funding from the Next Generation Learning Challenges (NGLC) initiative to support highly personalized approaches to learning. The study, conducted by RAND Corporation researchers for the Bill & Melinda Gates Foundation, compares the achievement of students in PL schools with (1) matched peers attending non-PL schools and (2) national norms. The study also compares achievement effects between charter and noncharter schools implementing PL.

What Is Personalized Learning, and How Does It Differ from Typical Practices?

To date, there is no single definition of PL. The research team distilled the following working definition based on conversations with practitioners and experts in the field:

> Personalized learning prioritizes a clear understanding of the needs and goals of each individual student and the tailoring of instruction to address those needs and goals. These needs and goals, and progress toward meeting them, are highly visible and easily accessible to teachers as well as students and their families, are frequently discussed among these parties, and are updated accordingly.

This aspiration contrasts with typical instructional approaches. In many U.S. schools, efforts to meet individual students' needs may take less priority than efforts to ensure that all students work toward grade-level standards, progress at the same pace as their grade-level peers, or prepare for grade-level tests at the end of the year. In a PL classroom, students' learning objectives, pace, and content are likely to vary to a greater extent than they would in a non-PL school. The idea behind PL is that personalized instructional approaches and strategies will improve student outcomes in the short term (e.g., stronger rates of growth in achievement) and in the long term (e.g., successful completion of a postsecondary degree or successful transition into a career).

Technology can play a role in supporting the complexity of the personalization process. When properly supported by teachers, it can help students learn independently and work at their own pace. Technology can also enable educators to take a more personalized approach in their teaching efforts and other activities they undertake to support student learning and development.

Personalized Learning Makes a Positive Difference in Mathematics Student Achievement

The research team analyzed mathematics and reading scores for approximately 5,500 students in 32 NGLC schools who took the Northwest Evaluation Association (NWEA) Measures of Academic Progress (MAP) mathematics and reading assessments for one academic year: fall 2014 to spring 2015. The team compared the NGLC MAP scores with the scores of students who did not attend NGLC schools, but who were otherwise similar to their NGLC peers in terms of gender, grade levels, starting test scores, and geographic locations.

The treatment effects were estimated to be approximately 0.09 in mathematics and 0.07 in reading. Only the mathematics estimate is statistically significant. The effect sizes translate to gains of about 3 percentile points; specifically, a student who would have performed at the median in the comparison group is estimated to have performed 3 percentile points above the median in an NGLC school in both math and reading.

Students Started Below National Norms, but Approached Them by the End of the Year

Students in the PL schools started the year significantly below national norms in both mathematics and reading, but moved closer to the norms during the school year. In mathematics, students gained about 2 percentile points but remained significantly below national norms; in reading, students also gained about 2 percentile points and were performing approximately at national norms by spring.

AI CONCERNS IN EDUCATION

If you're an educator, you've probably noticed that the profession has undergone significant change in the last few years.

With the growth of the flipped classroom model and the plethora of resources available via apps and websites, teachers are no longer considered the experts. They are moving into the role of facilitator, "guide on the side" instead of "sage on the stage."

In this context, some are beginning to wonder whether the expertise of face-to-face teachers is on its way to becoming obsolete in our schools.

Are we headed to a brave new world in which teachers are replaced by giant computer screens and a tech coach to assist on the sidelines?

The answer is...yes and no.

There is no doubt that many of the technological advances we've experienced have greatly simplified a teacher's job. It offers a wealth of tools for personalized learning, grading, and lesson planning, allowing teachers the time to interact with students in a more meaningful way. In addition, they have access to a dizzying repertoire of online videos which expose students to first-hand experiences and content area experts that they would never be able to encounter otherwise.

Personalized Learning Students Surpassed National Norms After Two Years

There were 16 NGLC schools that had been in operation the prior year, 2013–14, and had administered the MAP assessment in both academic years. To examine growth trajectories in those schools, the research team restricted the sample to students with test scores in fall and spring of both academic years and examined their scores relative to national norms.

In both mathematics and reading, cumulative growth over the two years is evident. Students started significantly below national norms, gained ground after one academic year, and gained further

But these advances are a double-edged sword. As teachers begin to rely more and more on such resources, their own expertise begins to feel less valuable. In the past, they were the ones with all the answers. Now, they are guiding students to find the answers on their own, a job that could just as easily be accomplished by a lowly "techie," hovering in the background.

Teachers are expensive.

They require a professional salary and benefits. All these costs for multiple teachers can add up. As schools try to become more economical, some wonder if educational technology could lessen the burden. It seems more economical to connect 50 students with one video lecturer than to connect just 25 with one traditional teacher.

Students may be digital natives, but they still need help in locating and using digital resources for learning. Teachers may no longer be valued as content-area experts, but they can help students learn how to build knowledge for themselves from the excess of tools and information that exists.

The best teachers care about us and inspire us to do our best. And that will never go out of style.

"Artificial Intelligence: Are Computers Taking Over for Teachers?" by Matthew Lynch, Matthew Lynch, September 23, 2017.

ground the second academic year, placing them above (though not statistically significantly above) national norms at the end of two years. The largest gains on average appeared to occur in the second year. This suggests that PL systems may require some experience before operating at their fullest potential.

Personalized Learning May Benefit Students of All Abilities

The research team also examined the fraction of NGLC students who surpassed comparison students in mathematics and reading achievement during the academic year. The students were divided into five groups based on their starting levels of achievement. Across the achievement spectrum, more than half of NGLC students surpassed their comparison students.

These results suggest that PL is benefiting students of all levels of prior achievement. For the lowest four groups, approximately 60 percent of NGLC students surpassed their comparison students in both mathematics and reading; for the highest group, the percentages are in the mid-50s.

Charter Schools Showed Bigger Gains Than Schools Operated by Districts

The average positive achievement effects are composed of widely varying estimates for individual schools. A slight majority of schools were estimated to have positive effects, but a few schools were estimated to have large negative effects on student achievement.

Eight NGLC schools in the achievement sample were operated by school districts; the remaining 24 were charter schools. The district schools were all high schools and middle schools, whereas the charter schools included schools serving all grade levels. This analysis calculated the average treatment effects for district and charter schools separately.

The charter schools performed similarly in both mathematics and reading, with estimated effects near 0.10.

The district schools have smaller estimates in both subjects, and the reading estimate is near zero. Due to the small sample of schools, the district estimates are particularly imprecise. This imprecision, coupled with the differences in the grade levels served by the two groups, indicates that these trends in district versus charter schools should be treated as suggestive but not conclusive.

Two Studies: Positive Results That Vary in Different School Contexts

The results for the 2017 study,[1] discussed above, demonstrated that PL has a slightly positive effect on student learning. Yet, a 2015 study showed larger gains.[2]

Why are the results from the two studies so different? Much of the difference is likely due to different study samples. The schools in the 2017 report were mostly secondary schools that were relatively new to implementing PL. The schools included in the 2015 report, on average, had greater experience in implementing PL and were primarily elementary schools. Because of these differences, the results of the two studies are not directly comparable.

Implications

Together, these analyses offer implications for districts and schools interested in or already implementing PL to consider as they move forward.

PL appears to be promising for improving student achievement. The early evidence presented here suggests that PL approaches can help improve achievement for a broad range of students. However, these results must be confirmed using more-rigorous experimental study designs. Moreover, the implementation of PL in schools is still in the early stages of development, and it is not clear what PL practices or combination of practices have the greatest impact.

PL effects differ across contexts. The positive results on average are composed of widely varying estimates for individual schools, including some schools that showed large negative effects. Other publications in this series describe challenges to PL implementation, which may be greater in certain contexts.

The full effects of PL may take some time to emerge. The benefits suggested by two-year analyses suggest that effects are more positive after schools have at least one year of experience implementing PL. It is not yet clear how effects will accumulate over longer durations, as schools and students gain experience with this major change to schooling. As the field matures with greater understanding of effective PL strategies and more-complete packages of curriculum materials and supports, larger and more-consistent positive effects may be possible. Removal of policy barriers that inhibit PL could also contribute to more-complete implementation.

Notes

[1] John F. Pane, Elizabeth D. Steiner, Matthew D. Baird, Laura S. Hamilton, and Joseph D. Pane, Informing Progress: Insights on Personalized Learning Implementation and Effects, Santa Monica, Calif.: RR-2042-BMGF, 2017 (available at www.rand. org/t/ RR2042).

[2] John F. Pane, Elizabeth D. Steiner, Matthew D. Baird, and Laura S. Hamilton, Continued Progress: Promising Evidence on Personalized Learning, Santa Monica, Calif.: RAND Corporation, RR-1365-BMGF, 2015 (available at www.rand.org/t/ RR1365).

> *"Personalized learning, which transforms education from a factory model to student-centered education, is demonstrating success with students of all backgrounds and abilities."*

Personalized Learning Has Positive Effects

Bob Nilsson

In the following viewpoint, Bob Nilsson argues that personalized learning occurs when a student's strengths, needs, and interests are taken into consideration, particularly through the use of competency-based progression, personal learning paths, and optimal instruction delivery (e.g., blended learning). Nilsson notes the contrasts between individualized learning and what he refers to as "factory schooling" in the traditional classroom, and points to the importance of the "Four Cs" as students make their way through their education: communication, collaboration, critical thinking, and creativity. Success in personalized learning can happen, but it depends on these factors and many more. Nilsson is the director of solutions marketing at Extreme Networks.

"Personalized Learning: Where It Came From, Why It Works, and How to Implement It," by Bob Nilsson, October 5, 2015. With permission of Extreme Network, Inc. Please visit Extreme Networks.com/K12.

As you read, consider the following questions:

1. What are some uses of the term "personalized learning," according to the author?
2. How do the concepts of personalized learning compare between K–12, higher education, and professional development?
3. What will the significance of interactive content be in the context of personalized learning, going forward?

Noah has completed a lesson in his digital math text book and is now working a series of problems. His answer to the first is accepted and he is presented with a second problem that he doesn't recognize. When he gets the answer wrong, a new explanatory passage appears followed by a slightly different version of the problem. Noah correctly answers this one and moves on to the next question. Later on in the lesson, Noah will be tested on the class of problem he got wrong a moment ago, just to make sure he fully understands it.

For his reading lesson, Mason selects a passage on rock music, one of his favorite topics. When he completes the article, he is presented with an assignment matched to his skill and interest.

Amelia not only tore through her evolutionary biology lesson, but demonstrated that she understood the content by acing all of the end of lesson questions. Wasting no time, she was happy to launch right in to a supplemental biology lesson that will help her with the biology advanced placement test that she is considering taking at the end of the year.

Olivia had struggled with the geometry lesson that she watched last night. Although she had done well up to this point, a key concept of an earlier lesson is now eluding her and the proofs she is working through are not making sense. Olivia's classroom teacher is made aware of Olivia's plight and the nature of the problems she is struggling with. In this case, the teacher has some ideas to share with Olivia to help her through these problems. As backup, the teacher's notebook *is aware of Olivia's struggle and is ready to assist the teacher with supplemental lessons and problems to share.*

Judy is sitting in a large classroom surrounded by her classmates, all of whom are 15 minutes into a 110-minute testing session. The first section of the test assesses Judy's knowledge of language and conventions, and she feels confident that she did well on it. But the second section on written expression has been painful. The class time spent on this material had not been enjoyable and Judy now wishes she hadn't been texting during those classes. Still, at the time, she thought she understood the content; but now she is unable to answer most of the questions on this portion of the test. Her mind is frozen with the possibility of failing the entire test, and possibly failing English, due to this one section, even though she knows all the other sections cold.

Noah, Mason, Amelia, and Olivia are participating in examples of different forms of personalized learning. Not all of these styles of learning are appropriate for all students. On the other hand, Judy's situation, which is still faced by far too many students, is optimal for none.

What Is Personalized Learning?

The term personalized learning has been used to describe everything from evolved teaching skills, enhanced curricula, and simple classroom segmentation, to breakthrough digital technologies delivered in ultra-futuristic learning spaces requiring ground-breaking teacher dexterity. The International Association for K-12 Online Learning (iNACOL), a focal point for the concept, describes personalized learning as:

Tailoring learning to each student's strengths, needs and interests—including enabling student voice and choice in what, how, when, and where they learn—to provide flexibility and supports to ensure mastery of the highest standards possible. This definition encapsulates all three major elements:

1. Competency-based progression to ensure that students advance at the rate that they master each subject

2. Personal learning paths, based on background, interests, strengths, motivations
3. Optimal instruction delivery blending personal student-teacher interaction with online digital content

Contrast this individualized style with factory schooling of the last-century: students aligned in rows, learning the facts and skills of arithmetic, history, and writing. The system filled the needs of the industrial era economy with graduates who could tabulate, record, calculate, schedule, measure, and manage. The theory was one size could fulfill all requirements. The only form of personalization during this era was to hold some students back a year for a repetition of the same content, taught in exactly the same manner each time.

Many of the skills taught in that earlier era are now routinely handled by computers at rates exceeding human capabilities by thousands of times. For example, the AP produces nearly 4,300 earnings articles per quarter without any human intervention. In fact, computers can write 10,000 articles in less than half the time it takes a human reporter to write one.

Students in our schools today will be offered careers that do not even exist yet. These new professions will require proficiency in the four Cs (Communication, Collaboration, Critical Thinking, and Creativity), rather than the three Rs (Reading, Writing, and Arithmetic) of yesterday.

Where Did Personalized Learning Come From?

Although there were vestiges of personalized learning as early as the 19th century, the current connotation and usage began about ten years ago. When the term was used in a 2004 speech by David Miliband, Minister of State for School Standards for the United Kingdom, the technology necessary for its implementation was starting to emerge. Educators experimenting with personalized learning were finding that their students became dramatically more engaged. Teachers observed that students with diverse experiences and backgrounds, including but not limited to different economic and cultural circumstances, responded differently to a range of techniques, examples, and styles. A theory developed that the learners' own contexts, including prior experiences, current interests, and future aspirations could be used to address learning challenges.

The Christensen Institute introduced the concept of blended learning, which incorporates education technology to give students more control over time, place, path, and pace of lessons. As an important side benefit, the technology made it possible to analyze which techniques work best for individual students.

The concepts of personalized learning are equally important for K-12, higher education, and even professional development. Students arriving on the college campus not only have a widely-varying cultural background, but may have different subject mastery that needs be identified and credited.

Personalized Learning, Online Learning, Flipped Learning, and Blended Learning

While personalized learning can be implemented without technology, it is dramatically more effective when combined with digital and adaptive capabilities. Recorded lectures make possible flipped learning, where students view lecture content outside of the classroom, leaving classroom time for personal interaction with the teacher. Segmenting lessons into on-line classes enables students to progress through modules at their own rate. Combining these styles provides a blended learning environment with both online lessons and in-person teacher discussions.

How Do We Know That Personalized Learning Works?

Beyond the intuitive feel that personalized learning makes sense, there is growing quantitative evidence of its effectiveness. A RAND Corporation study of 23 charter schools across the US found significant improvement in math and reading achievement resulting from personalized learning. All groups in the study showed large achievement growth; the group aged 7-8 actually doubled their ranking nationally from the 33% to the 64%.

The Institute of Personalized Learning reported growth in reading and math achievement nearly double what was expected after a pilot of 34 early elementary classrooms incorporated elements of personalized learning into the curriculum. The Christensen Institute has documented a dozen case studies with quantitative benefits attributable to personalized and blended learning. Among these are:

- District of Columbia Public Schools recorded extensive and well-studied student gains in math and reading on district-wide assessments
- Mooresville Graded School District was rated number one in North Carolina for meeting the state's targets for proficiency and other measures after implementing blended learning
- Washington County School District graduation rate improved from 80% in 2012 to 88% in 2014 with personalized learning
- Fraser Public Schools began implementing personalized learning in 2013 and reports "increased participation, lower achievement gaps, increased graduation rates, deeper learning, decreased truancy, increased digital fluency, and a tendency toward lifelong learning"

Is There a Downside to Personalized Learning?

If personalized learning is really the solution to the woes of education, why hasn't it already been implemented? Aside from the fact that all changes take time, there are indeed obstacles and even some drawbacks. The major hurdles involve resources and training. Schools are typically severely constrained by budget, so programs requiring new resources must be phased in over time.

The demands on the classroom teacher can rise with personalized learning. Whereas in the past a teacher could at least theoretically teach an entire class the same material synchronously, the very point of personalized learning is to individually assist students who are at different stages of understanding the content. Technology provides some assistance, but for success, the teacher must be capable of continually assessing each individual's understanding of the subjects in order to provide the appropriate coaching toward full comprehension.

What about the risk of students coming to school lacking motivation or even the ability to progress at a steady pace through their subjects? Learning and thinking is often hard. Not everyone will be able to assume the full responsibility demanded by personalized learning. Also, with class members by definition out of synch with each other, do group discussions and debates become impossible?

Since personalized learning increases engagement, student motivation, which is important throughout education, is at least as high as with traditional learning. In some cases, students who demonstrate competency early can be rewarded with free discretionary time, as a powerful motivator. If student does experience a setback or lull in energy, it tends to be easier to spot and correct with personalized learning.

In practice, personalized learning easily incorporates group activities and debates. In fact, the collaborative group project has become an important characteristic of the personalized learning experience.

What Elements Are Needed for Successful Personalized Learning?

Personalized learning benefits tremendously from digital content. This includes digital text books, video lectures, experiments and field trips. Lecture and video-capture software helps record and organize content presentation. Digital content needs to be presented through student devices, such as eReaders, tablets and notebooks. Usage of Chromebooks with their centralized management, collaborative apps and durability is growing and expected to comprise about half of all student devices in the classroom. New content such as augmented reality and virtual reality require special headsets. A rock-solid Wi-Fi and wired network insures the digital content is delivered as needed.

The next step beyond simple digital media is interactive content that tracks the student's understanding and either accelerates progress or provides review and supplemental lessons to insure subject competency. This includes adaptive learning technology that assesses student progress through in-line quizzes, by monitoring the student's path and speed, and by tracking how many hints are offered and accepted.

Emerging applications and software are rapidly advancing the possibilities of personalized learning. Software platforms that incorporate adaptive and competency-based learning systems help relieve some of the new burden from the classroom teacher. Open Educational Resources (OER), such as OER Commons can be a rich source of personalized learning content. Formative assessment software, which can be as simple as Google Forms, can be used to ascertain individual comprehension. Strategic simulation games have come a long way from the now-archaically-droning drill and skill style of the early education game programs. Learning Management Systems (LMS), such as Moodle, Blackboard, and Jenzabar provide individual student tracking.

Traditional classrooms can certainly be used for personalized learning, but some districts are taking the concept further and creating collaborative learning spaces. The ideal environment for personalized learning provides flexibility for students to work together in small groups or individually with a teacher. Walls are extended white boards for drawing and flat panel displays which can be connected to any student or teacher device are distributed around the rooms. Designated classrooms may be turned into makerspaces or creative areas for tinkering and building may be distributed throughout your schools. See our round-up blog for more on educational technology products for personalized learning.

The Role of Online Testing

While online testing is not required for personalized learning, it has an emerging role; that is not related to high-stakes testing. Common Core, which has received so much negative political attention, also involves online formative testing. The two consortia that have developed Common Core online summative tests are now developing formative tools to help teachers understand how well students understand the curriculum as they progress through it. Here is a glimpse of their summative assessment work: Partnership For Assessment Of Readiness For College And Careers (PARCC) and the Smarter Balanced Assessment Consortium.

Getting Started

Good research and planning is the best way to get started. Wisconsin's School District of Elmbrook started with a regional study of districts implementing personalized learning practices so they could learn from others and build a support network as they progressed. Professional development for all the teachers involved is critical prior to launch. Personalized learning brings new challenges to the teachers, so it is vital that they be well-prepared.

School districts that have successfully transitioned to personalized learning emphasize the cultural change required. Superintendent Dr. David Richards of Fraser Public Schools and Director of Educational Technology & Information Systems Troy Lindner note that they had to educate two generations at once as their district moved to personalized learning. The concepts involved were just as new to the parents of the community as they were to the students. Richards and Lidner started with an iPad one-to-one computing program and held a series of parents' nights to prepare them as they transitioned away from paper to online content.

Make sure your technology infrastructure can handle the increased digital loading. A solid Wi-Fi network will be needed to support the density and flexibility required for the student devices in each classroom space.

Consider moving to non-traditional grading standards. Competency-based education insures that all students will achieve mastery, so a system with a range of letter grades no longer makes sense. New competency-based grading policies are emerging as alternatives to time-based or letter-based systems.

As with all major program changes, start with a pilot, evaluate and communicate the results, make adjustments, and when ready, roll the full program out across the district.

Advancing the State of Personalized Learning Through Investment and Research

The need to improve education as reflected in international assessments such as the Program for International Student Assessment (PISA), as well as persistent achievement gaps among students from different economic circumstances and backgrounds has motivated charitable organizations including the Bill & Melinda Gates Foundation and the Michael & Susan Dell Foundation to dedicate resources to personalized learning. The most recent PISA test ranking of US students puts US math scores below the midpoint of the world's most-developed countries.

The Bill & Melinda Gates Foundation has invested to "identify, strengthen, and refine promising personalized learning practices; determine which are most effective; and encourage innovative educators and other leaders to spread the most successful practices to other classrooms, schools, and districts." Ongoing grants toward personalized learning by the Gates Foundation focus on these areas: Schools & Systems, Digital Tools & Content, and Building Capacity In Schools & Districts.

At almost $700M, Education-related grants make up two-thirds of the Dell Foundation donations. Their Personalized Learning Blog shares best practices and results from around the country. Grants by the Dell Foundation focus on Performance-Driven Education and Blended Learning.

Conclusion

Personalized learning, which transforms education from a factory model to student-centered education, is demonstrating success with students of all backgrounds and abilities. Getting there requires planning, professional development, technology, infrastructure, and ultimately new collaborative classroom designs. Along the way it demands a new culture within the educational community, one that embraces student responsibility for learning while providing individual paths leading to content mastery of all subjects.

> *"Over the last 30 years or so, skill-biased technological change has fueled the polarization of both employment and wages, with median workers facing real wage stagnation and non-college-educated workers suffering a significant decline in their real earnings."*

The True Impact of Automation on the Future of Jobs Remains Unclear

Laura D'Andrea Tyson

In the following viewpoint, Laura D'Andrea Tyson argues that the bulk of manufacturing job losses in the United States in the past 30 years have been a result of technological change and automation, and not about trade, as President Donald Trump's administration has presented. The author discusses the possibility of both a jobless future and a good-jobless future, or a bit of a combination of the two, which is, she believes, more likely. She also discusses the relationship between technological change and globalization, both of which impact employment, wages, and income inequality. Tyson is the interim dean at the University of California, Berkeley, Haas School of Business.

"The Future Is Automated, but What Does That Really Mean for Jobs?" by Laura D'Andrea Tyson, World Economic Forum, June 13, 2017. Reprinted by permission.

As you read, consider the following questions:

1. According to economists, what has been the primary reason for job loss in recent years?
2. What kinds of jobs are needed less as automation becomes more prevalent?
3. What does the author believe will maximize the benefits of smart machines?

Advances in artificial intelligence and robotics are powering a new wave of automation, with machines matching or outperforming humans in a fast-growing range of tasks, including some that require complex cognitive capabilities and advanced degrees. This process has outpaced the expectations of experts; not surprisingly, its possible adverse effects on both the quantity and quality of employment have raised serious concerns.

To listen to President Donald Trump's administration, one might think that trade remains the primary reason for the loss of manufacturing jobs in the United States. Trump's treasury secretary, Steven Mnuchin, has declared that the possible technological displacement of workers is "not even on [the administration's] radar screen."

Among economists, however, the consensus is that about 80% of the loss in US manufacturing jobs over the last three decades was a result of labor-saving and productivity-enhancing technological change, with trade coming a distant second. The question, then, is whether we are headed toward a jobless future, in which technology leaves many unemployed, or a "good-jobless future," in which a growing number of workers can no longer earn a middle-class income, regardless of their education and skills.

The answer may be some of both. The most recent major study on the topic found that, from 1990 to 2007, the penetration of industrial robots—defined as autonomous, automatically controlled, reprogrammable, and multipurpose machines—undermined both employment and wages.

Based on the study's simulations, robots probably cost about 400,000 US jobs each year, many of them middle-income manufacturing jobs, especially in industries like automobiles, plastics, and pharmaceuticals. Of course, as a recent Economic Policy Institute report points out, these are not large numbers, relative to the overall size of the US labor market. But local job losses have had an impact: many of the most affected communities were in the Midwestern and southern states that voted for Trump, largely because of his protectionist, anti-trade promises.

As automation substitutes for labor in a growing number of occupations, the impact on the quantity and quality of jobs will intensify. And, as a recent McKinsey Global Institute study shows, there is plenty more room for such substitution. The study, which encompassed 46 countries and 80% of the global labor force, found that relatively few occupations—less than 5%—could be fully automated. But some 60% of all occupations could have at least 30% of their constitutive tasks or activities automated, based on current demonstrated technologies.

The activities most susceptible to automation in the near term are routine cognitive tasks like data collection and data processing, as well as routine manual and physical activities in structured, predictable environments. Such activities now account for 51% of US wages, and are most prevalent in sectors that employ large numbers of workers, including hotel and food services, manufacturing, and retail trade.

The McKinsey report also found a negative correlation between tasks' wages and required skill levels on the one hand, and the potential for their automation on the other. On balance, automation reduces demand for low- and middle-skill labor in lower-paying routine tasks, while increasing demand for high-skill, high-earning labor performing abstract tasks that require technical and problem-solving skills. Simply put, technological change is skill-biased.

Over the last 30 years or so, skill-biased technological change has fueled the polarization of both employment and wages, with median workers facing real wage stagnation and non-college-educated workers suffering a significant decline in their real earnings. Such polarization fuels rising inequality in the distribution of labor income, which in turn drives growth in overall income inequality—a dynamic that many economists, from David Autor to Thomas Piketty, have emphasized.

As Michael Spence and I argue in a recent paper, skill-biased and labor-displacing intelligent machines and automation drive income inequality in several other ways, including winner-take-all effects that bring massive benefits to superstars and the luckiest few, as well as rents from imperfect competition and first-mover advantages in networked systems. Returns to digital capital tend to exceed the returns to physical capital and reflect power-law distributions, with an outsize share of returns again accruing to relatively few actors.

Technological change, Spence and I point out, has also had another inequality-enhancing consequence: it has "turbo-charged" globalization by enabling companies to source, monitor, and coordinate production processes at far-flung locations quickly and cheaply, in order to take advantage of lower labor costs. Given this, it is difficult to distinguish between the effects of technology and the effects of globalization on employment, wages, and income inequality in developed countries.

Our analysis concludes that the two forces reinforce each other, and have helped to fuel the rise in capital's share of national income—a key variable in Piketty's theory of wealth inequality. The April 2017 IMF World Economic Outlook reaches a similar conclusion, attributing about 50% of the 30-year decline in labor's share of national income in the developed economies to the impact of technology. Globalization, the IMF estimates, contributed about half that much to the decline.

Mounting anxiety about the potential effects of increasingly intelligent tools on employment, wages, and income inequality has led to calls for policies to slow the pace of automation, such as a tax on robots. Such policies, however, would undermine innovation and productivity growth, the primary force behind rising living standards.

Rather than cage the golden goose of technological progress, policymakers should focus on measures that help those who are displaced, such as education and training programs, and income support and social safety nets, including wage insurance, lifetime retraining loans, and portable health and pension benefits. More progressive tax and transfer policies will also be needed, in order to ensure that the income and wealth gains from automation are more equitably shared.

Three years ago, I argued that whether the benefits of smart machines are distributed broadly will depend not on their design, but on the design of the policies surrounding them. Since then, I have not been alone. Unfortunately, Trump's team hasn't gotten the message.

| "*By our calculations there is, as yet, essentially no visible relationship between the use of robots and the change in manufacturing employment.*"

Robots Are Improving Productivity, Not Costing Jobs

Mark Muro and Scott Andes

In the following viewpoint, Mark Muro and Scott Andes argue that the impact of robots and automation on productivity is not as clear cut as it is often presented. While losses of jobs have been reported, the final, net numbers don't necessarily correlate to the events often named as being responsible for the drops. Muro is a senior fellow and policy director at the Metropolitan Policy Program at Brookings. Andes is a former senior policy analyst and associate fellow at the Brookings Institution's Anne T. and Robert M. Bass Initiative on Innovation and Placemaking and currently program director of the National League of Cities.

"Robots Seem to Be Improving Productivity, Not Costing Jobs," by Mark Muro and Scott Andes, Harvard Business School Publishing, June 16, 2015. Reprinted by permission.

As you read, consider the following questions:

1. What have productivity statistics in recent years looked like?
2. What kinds of jobs do Graetz and Michaels see increasing with the onset of increased automation?
3. What "experience" do the authors point to as an indicator of how long it may take for industries to fully adopt automation?

Nearly 30 years ago, in 1987, the Nobel-winning economist Robert Solow surveyed the impact of IT on the economy and concluded that "you can see the computer age everywhere but in the productivity statistics."

Solow's quip crystallized a frustrating disconnect in the 1980s. Why did an observed technology boom coincide with a prolonged slump in the productivity data? Companies were using computers, but they didn't seem to be getting any more productive.

Strangely, it took another seven years for U.S. productivity growth to surge. At last, the computers Solow and everyone else saw around them had become visible in the statistics. It just took a while.

Well, here we go again. Now robots are everywhere—but they are also an object of confusion.

In early April the think tank Third Way published research by Henry Siu and Nir Jaimovich that blamed robots and automation for the fact that many repetitive jobs have all but vanished from the economic recovery. And yet, as Larry Summers noted recently, for all of the anecdotal evidence that automation is prompting mass layoffs and presumably increasing productivity, the "productivity statistics over the last dozen years are dismal."

Again, something is failing to compute. And what's more, the fact that there hasn't been much macroeconomic research on the impact of robots has only added to the confusion. Commentators have largely been forced to rely on anecdote.

However, empirical evidence is beginning to trickle in that could begin to clear up the current paradox. Provided in a new paper from London's Center for Economic Research, the analysis offered by George Graetz and Guy Michaels of Uppsala University and the London School of Economics, respectively, offers some of the first rigorous macroeconomic research and finds that industrial robots have been a substantial driver of labor productivity and economic growth.

To fuel their analysis, Graetz and Michaels employ new data from the International Federation of Robotics to analyze the use of industrial robots across 14 industries in 17 countries between 1993 and 2007. What do they find? Overall, Graetz and Michaels conclude that the use of robots within manufacturing raised the annual growth of labor productivity and GDP by 0.36 and 0.37 percentage points, respectively, between 1993 and 2007. That might not seem like a lot but it represents 10% of total GDP growth in the countries studied and 16% of labor productivity growth over that time period.

Moreover, to put that gain in context, it's worth noting that the robots' contribution to productivity growth in the 1990s and 2000s is comparable to that of a true "general purpose technology" (GPT) —one that has a pervasive, longstanding impact on a number of dissimilar industries. Graetz and Michaels calculate, for example, that robotics have of late increased labor productivity by about 0.35% annually—or by about the same amount as did the steam engine, a classic example of a GPT, during the years 1850 to 1910.

More recently, other analysis has shown that the pervasive IT revolution supported 0.60% of labor productivity growth and 1.0% of overall growth in Europe, the U.S., and Japan between 1995 and 2005. That's about two to three times the amount contributed by robotics thus far but capital investment rates in IT during those years were also five times higher than those in industrial robots during the 1993 to 2007 period. As many economists have noted, productivity figures are often quite difficult to calculate in new technology categories, and could be larger or smaller than official estimates. Nonetheless, to the extent that one can trust today's flawed productivity data, Graetz and Michaels' work suggests the young robotics revolution is going to be a very big deal.

And yet, there is another critical question that needs asking, and that is whether the robots' productivity impacts are resulting in job losses.

Consider that between 1993 and 2007 (the timeframe studied by Graetz and Michaels) the U.S. increased the number of robots in use as a portion of the total hours of manufacturing work (a standard measure of economic output) by 237%. During the same period the U.S. economy shed 2.2 million manufacturing jobs.

So is there a relationship between the use of industrial robots and job loss? The substantial variation of the degree to which countries deploy robots according to Graetz' and Michaels' data should provide clues. If robots are a substitute for human workers, then one would expect the countries with higher investment rates in automation to have experienced greater employment loss in their manufacturing sectors. For example, Germany deploys over three times as many robots per hour worked than the U.S., according to Graetz and Michaels, largely due to Germany's robust automotive industry, which is by far the most robot-intensive industry (with over 10 times more robots per worker than the average industry). Sweden has 60% more robots per hours worked than the U.S. thanks to its highly technical metal and chemical industries.

However, these data don't compute with expectations. By our calculations there is, as yet, essentially no visible relationship between the use of robots and the change in manufacturing employment. Despite the installation of far more robots between 1993 and 2007, Germany lost just 19% of its manufacturing jobs between 1996 and 2012 compared to a 33% drop in the U.S. (We introduce a three-year time lag to allow for robots to influence the labor market and continued with the most recent data, 2012). Korea, France, and Italy also lost fewer manufacturing jobs than the United States, even as they introduced more industrial robots. On the other hand, countries like the United Kingdom and

Australia invested less in robots but saw faster declines in their manufacturing sectors.

For their part, Graetz and Michaels also see a lot of ambiguity when it comes to robotics' influence on the labor force. They cannot rule out that there is no effect of robot densification on national employment levels. But they do see variegated skill-biased impacts. Specifically, their data suggest that the arrival of robots tended to increase the employment and pay of skilled workers even as it seemed to "crowd out" employment of low-skill and, to a lesser extent, middle-skill workers. So while robots don't seem to be causing net job losses, they do seem to change the sort of workers that are in demand.

In the end, the new data are important because they dispel at least some of the robotics productivity paradox. Assuming more analyses fall into line with Graetz' and Michael's work it will be possible to say that robots have become visible in the productivity data—and that the data and observed realities match up and can be useful. In addition, the scale of the robots' impact—even with technology improvements racing along—suggests that robotics may well be a big thing: a general purpose technology that over time pervades the economy, spawns myriad new innovations, and elevates productivity for years, with major impacts on society. No, we're not there yet, as Summers notes, but the evidence suggests that day is coming. As to the bots' impact on employment, that is less clearly visible, and may be positive, negative, or mixed. Yet if the IT experience is any indicator, full adoption of a powerful technology can take a generation, and come after years of delay. In that sense, while it's early, the advent of the robots is beginning to conform to expectations.

Periodical and Internet Sources Bibliography

The following articles have been selected to supplement the diverse views presented in this chapter.

Timothy B. Lee, "Automation Is Making Human Labor More Valuable Than Ever," vox.com, September 16, 2016. vox.com/a/new -economy-future/manual-labor-luxury-good.

Anthony Melanson, "How Robotic Automation Is Changing the Job Market," aethon.com, 2018. aethon.com/robotic-automation-is -changing-the-job-market.

David Rotman, "The Relentless Pace of Automation," TechnologyReview.com, February 13, 2017. technologyreview .com/s/603465/the-relentless-pace-of-automation.

James Sherk, "The Rise of the 'Gig' Economy: Good for Workers and Consumers," heritage.org, October 7, 2016. heritage.org/jobs -and-labor/report/the-rise-the-gig-economy-good-workers-and -consumers.

Harriet Taylor, "How Robots Will Kill the 'Gig Economy,'" cnbc.com, March 9, 2016. cnbc.com/2016/03/09/how-robots-will-kill-the -gig-economy.html.

Sorina Teleanu, "The Future of Work: Preparing for automation and the gig economy," diplomacy.edu, March 25, 2018. diplomacy .edu/blog/future-work-preparing-automation-and-gig-economy.

Adam C. Uzialko, "How Will Business Automation Impact Workers in the Gig Economy?," BusinessNewsDaily.com, May 16, 2017. businessnewsdaily.com/9939-business-automation-gig-economy -workers.html.

Jamie Woodcock, "Automate This! Delivering Resistance in the Gig Economy," metamute.org, March 10, 2017. metamute.org /editorial/articles/automate-delivering-resistance-gig-economy.

Tom Watson, "When Robots Do All the Work, How Will People Live?," theguardian.com, March 8, 2016. theguardian.com /commentisfree/2016/mar/08/robots-technology-industrial -strategy.

CHAPTER 4

Are We Headed Toward a Jobless Future?

Chapter Preface

When the current evolution of technology is compared to the Industrial Revolution, it can be argued that automation of labor is a shift not unlike economic and technological changes that have already taken place.

However, the much faster pace and far deeper scope of the changes that result from increases in automated labor create an apples-and-oranges situation, where we are not really comparing two "like" concepts. With that in mind, the automation of labor may indeed pose a serious threat to the employability of our population.

In this chapter, we take a look at both sides of this debate. Society can count on technological advances being unpredictable, and they can expect the increased productivity that results from such advances to generate economic growth. And even with the threat—as some believe it is—of automation leading to job loss, one author points to the bigger concern of a human threat: those who are willing to do the same work as current employees, but for lower wages. While some experts believe concerns about AI amount to not much more than fear mongering, others are sincere in their belief that AI may truly be a threat to the jobs of the future.

One concern for the future is rooted in results some people are seeing today, although it is also accepted as what could be considered collateral damage of capitalism—the fact that higher productivity often does not lead to higher pay for the individuals who are making it happen, other than those all the way at the top. With this result in mind, workers are demonstrating higher output and delivering higher numbers of products (and even services), without seeing a reflection of that in their paycheck. Ultimately, there is a real fear—among some—that the future is bleak, while others see a silver lining to the current path of progress.

| *"Two-thirds of Americans think it's likely that in 50 years robots and computers will do much of the work currently done by humans."*

Workers Express Concerns About the Future of Their Jobs

Aaron Smith

In the following viewpoint, Aaron Smith argues that while people in the workforce are worried about being replaced by robots or their jobs becoming automated, they are more concerned about being replaced by a person who will work for a lower salary and fewer or no benefits. He cites a range of reasons why people are concerned they might lose their jobs, from management issues to industry-wide concerns, to technical skills and more. The bulk of people with these concerns are individuals whose jobs include manual labor. Aaron Smith is associate director of research on internet and technology issues at Pew Research Center.

"Public Predictions for the Future of Workforce Automation," by Aaron Smith, Pew Research Center, March 10, 2016.

As you read, consider the following questions:

1. What are some of the reasons people are concerned their jobs are at risk of being eliminated?
2. Describe the differences in jobs of people who are most to least concerned about their own job security.
3. People in what job categories or industries express the least amount of concern that their jobs are at risk?

From self-driving vehicles and semi-autonomous robots to intelligent algorithms and predictive analytic tools, machines are increasingly capable of performing a wide range of jobs that have long been human domains. A 2013 study by researchers at Oxford University posited that as many as 47% of all jobs in the United States are at risk of "computerization." And many respondents in a recent Pew Research Center canvassing of technology experts predicted that advances in robotics and computing applications will result in a net displacement of jobs over the coming decades—with potentially profound implications for both workers and society as a whole.

The ultimate extent to which robots and algorithms intrude on the human workforce will depend on a host of factors, but many Americans expect that this shift will become reality over the next half-century. In a national survey by Pew Research Center conducted June 10-July 12, 2015, among 2,001 adults, fully 65% of Americans expect that within 50 years robots and computers will "definitely" or "probably" do much of the work currently done by humans.

Yet even as many Americans expect that machines will take over a great deal of human employment, an even larger share (80%) expect that their own jobs or professions will remain largely unchanged and exist in their current forms 50 years from now. And although 11% of today's workers are at least somewhat concerned that they might lose their jobs as a result of workforce automation, a larger number are occupied by more immediate worries—such as displacement by lower-paid human workers, broader industry trends or mismanagement by their employers.

Two-thirds of Americans think it's likely that in 50 years robots and computers will do much of the work currently done by humans

Government, education and nonprofit workers are slightly more skeptical about the likelihood of widespread workforce automation. When it comes to their general predictions for the future of human employment and workforce automation, roughly two-thirds of Americans expect that within the next 50 years robots and computers will do much of the work currently done by humans. Some 15% of Americans expect that this level of automation will "definitely" happen, while 50% think it will "probably" happen. On the other hand, one-quarter of Americans expect that this outcome will probably not happen, and 7% believe it will definitely not happen.

In general, Americans of various demographic backgrounds have largely similar expectations regarding the future of automation. However, those under the age of 50—as well as those with relatively high household incomes and levels of educational attainment—are a bit more skeptical than average about the likelihood of widespread workforce automation. Some 35% of 18- to 49-year-olds think it unlikely that robots and computers will do much of the work done by humans, compared with 27% of those ages 50 and older. And 37% of those with a college degree think that this outcome is unlikely (compared with 28% of those who have not attended college), as do 38% of Americans with an annual household income of $75,000 or more (compared with 27% of those with an annual household income of less than $30,000 per year).

Similarly, Americans who work in the government, nonprofit or education sectors are a bit more skeptical about the future of workforce automation than are Americans who work for a large corporation, medium-sized company or small business. Just 7% of Americans who work in the government, education or nonprofit

Ethical AI

The Information Technology Industry Council—a DC-based group representing the likes of IBM, Microsoft, Google, Amazon, Facebook and Apple—is today releasing principles for developing ethical artificial intelligence systems.

Why it matters: The tech industry is trying to get ahead of growing anxieties about the societal impact of AI technologies, and this is an acknowledgement on companies' part that their data-hungry products are causing sweeping changes in the way we work and live. The companies hope that pledging to handle this power responsibly will win points with critics in Washington, and that showing they can police themselves will help stave off government regulation on this front.

Why now: ITI President Dean Garfield said the industry has learned painful lessons by staying on the sidelines of past debates about technology-driven societal shifts. That's something the industry wants to avoid this time. "Sometimes our instinct is to just put our heads down and do our work, to develop, design and innovate," he told Axios. "But there's a recognition that our ability to innovate is going to be affected by how society perceives it."

The principles include:

- Ensure the responsible design and deployment of AI systems, including taking "steps to avoid the reasonably predictable misuse of this technology by committing to ethics by design."
- Promote the responsible use of data and test for potentially harmful bias in the deployment of AI systems.
- Commit to mitigating bias, inequity and other potential harms in automated decision-making systems.
- Commit to finding a "reasonable accountability framework" to address concerns about liability issues created when autonomous decision-making replaces decisions made by humans.

Other efforts: Last week, Intel laid out its own public policy principles for artificial intelligence, including setting aside R&D funds for testing the technologies and creating new human employment opportunities as AI changes the way people work. The biggest tech companies (as well as smaller AI firms) started the Partnership on AI, a non-profit aimed at developing industry best practices.

"Tech Companies Pledge to Use Artificial Intelligence Responsibly," by Kim Hart, AXIOS Media Inc, October 24, 2017.

sectors expect that robots and computers will definitely take over most human employment in the next 50 years, while 13% of those who work for a large corporation or small business or medium-sized company are certain that this will occur.

Despite their expectations that technology will encroach on human employment in general, most workers think that their own jobs or professions will still exist in 50 years

Yet even as most Americans expect significant levels of workforce and job automation to occur over the next 50 years, most of today's workers express confidence that their own jobs or occupations will not be impacted to a substantial degree. Fully 36% of workers anticipate that their current jobs or occupations will "definitely" exist in their current forms five decades from now, while an additional 44% expect that their jobs will "probably" exist in 50 years. Roughly one-in-five workers expect that their current jobs will "probably not" (12%) or "definitely not" (6%) exist in their current forms that far in the future.

Overall there are relatively few differences in these expectations based on workers' demographic characteristics, and the differences that do exist are relatively modest. For instance, younger workers are a bit more likely than older workers to expect that their current jobs will exist 50 years in the future: 84% of workers ages 18 to 29 expect that this will be the case, compared with 76% of workers ages 50 and older.

And as was the case for their predictions for workforce automation in general, workers in government, education and nonprofit sectors are a bit more confident than those in the private sector that their jobs will exist in their current forms 50 years from now: 86% of these workers expect that this will be the case (including 42% who indicate that their current jobs will "definitely" exist), compared with 79% of those who work for a large corporation, medium-sized company or small business.

Along with these differences based on place of employment, workers' views on this subject also differ somewhat based on the type of work they currently do. For instance, 41% of workers whose jobs involve mostly manual or physical labor expect that their current jobs will "definitely" exist in their current forms in 50 years, as do 34% of those who describe their current occupations as "professional." By contrast, just 23% of those who currently work in a managerial or executive role expect that their current jobs will exist unchanged for the next five decades. But overall, a substantial majority of workers across a range of categories express confidence in the long-term staying power of their current jobs or professions.

One-in-ten workers are concerned about losing their current jobs due to workforce automation, but competition from lower-paid human workers and broader industry trends pose a more immediate worry

Many Americans expect workforce automation to become much more prominent over the coming half-century, but relatively few of today's workers see computers and robots as an imminent threat to their job prospects at the moment.

When asked about a number of issues that might cause them to lose their current jobs, just 11% of workers are at least somewhat concerned that they might lose their jobs because their employer replaces human workers with machines or computer programs. On the other hand, roughly one-in-five express concern that they might lose their jobs because their employer finds other (human) workers to perform their jobs for less money or because their overall industry workforce is shrinking. The most prominent concern is poor management by their own employer, albeit by a narrow margin, among the five evaluated in this survey:

- 26% of workers are concerned that they might lose their current jobs because the company they work for is poorly managed.

- 22% are concerned about losing their jobs because their overall industry is shrinking.
- 20% are concerned that their employer might find someone who is willing to do their jobs for less money.
- 13% are concerned that they won't be able to keep up with the technical skills needed to stay competitive in their jobs.
- 11% are concerned that their employer might use machines or computer programs to replace human workers.

Workers whose jobs involve primarily manual or physical labor express heightened concern about all of these potential employment threats, especially when it comes to replacement by robots or other machines. Fully 17% of these workers are at least somewhat concerned about the threat from workforce automation, with 11% indicating that they are "very concerned." By contrast, just 5% of workers whose jobs do not involve manual labor express some level of concern about the threat of workforce automation.

"Somehow, we believe our livelihoods will be safe. They're not: every commercial sector will be affected by robotic automation in the next several years."

Robots May Lead to Employment Devastation

Dan Shewan

In the following viewpoint, Dan Shewan argues that robotic automation will have a profound impact on the workforce, which will go beyond the manufacturing tasks people have come to expect from robotic technology. He warns that advancements in areas directed at consumer markets, including motion control, sensor technologies, and artificial intelligence, will lead the charge for these changes. Shewan is a journalist who writes for a number of outlets, including the Guardian.

As you read, consider the following questions:

1. What is a "Create Your Taste" kiosk and how does it work?
2. What is the World Economic Forum's prediction for the future of robotics and their impact on employment in the US?
3. What is Simbe Robotics' robot, Tally, capable of handling, according to the author?

The McDonald's on the corner of Third Avenue and 58th Street in New York City doesn't look all that different from any of the fast-food chains other locations across the country. Inside, however, hungry patrons are welcomed not by a cashier waiting to take their order, but by a "Create Your Taste" kiosk—an automated touch-screen system that allows customers to create their own burgers without interacting with another human being.

It's impossible to say exactly how many jobs have been lost by the deployment of the automated kiosks—McDonald's has been predictably reluctant to release numbers—but such innovations will be an increasingly familiar sight in Trump's America.

Once confined to the pages of futuristic dystopian fictions, the field of robotics promises to be the most profoundly disruptive technological shift since the industrial revolution. While robots have been utilized in several industries, including the automotive and manufacturing sectors, for decades, experts now predict that a tipping point in robotic deployments is imminent—and that much of the developed world simply isn't prepared for such a radical transition.

Many of us recognize robotic automation as an inevitably disruptive force. However, in a classic example of optimism bias, while approximately two-thirds of Americans believe that robots will inevitably perform most of the work currently done by human beings during the next 50 years, about 80% also believe their current jobs will either "definitely" or "probably" exist in their current form within the same timeframe.

Somehow, we believe our livelihoods will be safe. They're not: every commercial sector will be affected by robotic automation in the next several years.

For example, Australian company Fastbrick Robotics has developed a robot, the Hadrian X, that can lay 1,000 standard bricks in one hour—a task that would take two human bricklayers the better part of a day or longer to complete.

In 2015, San Francisco-based startup Simbe Robotics unveiled Tally, a robot the company describes as "the world's first fully autonomous shelf auditing and analytics solution" that roams supermarket aisles alongside human shoppers during regular business hours and ensures that goods are adequately stocked, placed and priced.

Swedish agricultural equipment manufacturer DeLaval International recently announced that its new cow-milking robots will be deployed at a small family-owned dairy farm in Westphalia, Michigan, at some point later this year. The system allows cows to come and be milked on their own, when they please.

Data from the Robotics Industries Association (RIA), one of the largest robotic automation advocacy organizations in North America, reveals just how prevalent robots are likely to be in the workplace of tomorrow. During the first half of 2016 alone, North American robotics technology vendors sold 14,583 robots worth $817m to companies around the world. The RIA further estimates that more than 265,000 robots are currently deployed at factories across the country, placing the US third worldwide in terms of robotics deployments behind only China and Japan.

In a recent report, the World Economic Forum predicted that robotic automation will result in the net loss of more than 5m jobs across 15 developed nations by 2020, a conservative estimate. Another study, conducted by the International Labor Organization, states that as many as 137m workers across Cambodia, Indonesia, the Philippines, Thailand and Vietnam—approximately 56% of the total workforce of those countries—are at risk of displacement by robots, particularly workers in the garment manufacturing industry.

A Trump-Sized Problem

Advocates for robotic automation routinely point to the fact that, for the most part, robots cannot service or program themselves—yet. In theory, this will create new, high-skilled jobs for technicians, programmers and other newly essential roles.

However, for every job created by robotic automation, several more will be eliminated entirely. At scale, this disruption will have a devastating impact on our workforce.

Few people understand this tension better than Dr Jing Bing Zhang, one of the world's leading experts on the commercial applications of robotics technology. As research director for global marketing intelligence firm IDC, Zhang studies how commercial robotics is likely to shape tomorrow's workforce.

IDC's FutureScape: Worldwide Robotics 2017 Predictions report, authored by Zhang and his team, reveals the extent of the coming shift that will jeopardize the livelihoods of millions of people.

By 2018, the reports says, almost one-third of robotic deployments will be smarter, more efficient robots capable of collaborating with other robots and working safely alongside humans. By 2019, 30% or more of the world's leading companies will employ a chief robotics officer, and several governments around the world will have drafted or implemented specific legislation surrounding robots and safety, security and privacy. By 2020, average salaries in the robotics sector will increase by at least 60%—yet more than one-third of the available jobs in robotics will remain vacant due to shortages of skilled workers.

"Automation and robotics will definitely impact lower-skilled people, which is unfortunate," Zhang told me via phone from his office in Singapore. "I think the only way for them to move up or adapt to this change is not to hope that the government will protect their jobs from technology, but look for ways to retrain themselves. No one can expect to do the same thing for life. That's just not the case any more."

Meanwhile, developments in motion control, sensor technologies, and artificial intelligence will inevitably give rise to an entirely new class of robots aimed primarily at consumer markets—robots the likes of which we have never seen before. Upright, bipedal robots that live alongside us in our homes; robots that interact with us in increasingly sophisticated ways—in short, robots that were once the sole province of the realms of science fiction.

This, according to Zhang, represents an unparalleled opportunity for companies positioned to take advantage of this shift, yet it also poses significant challenges, such as the necessity of new regulatory frameworks to ensure our safety and privacy —precisely the kind of essential regulation that Trump spoke out against so vociferously on the campaign trail.

According to Zhang, the field of robotics actually favors what Trump pledged to do on the campaign trail—bring manufacturing back to the US. Unfortunately for Trump, robots won't help him keep another of his grandiose promises, namely creating new jobs for lower-skilled workers. The only way corporations can mitigate against increasing labor costs in the US without compromising on profit margins is to automate low-skilled jobs.

Time for a Career Change, Then?

With millions of jobs at risk and a worldwide employment crisis looming, it is only logical that we should turn to education as a way to understand and prepare for the robotic workforce of tomorrow. In an increasingly unstable employment market, developed nations desperately need more science, technology, engineering and math— commonly abbreviated as Stem—graduates to remain competitive.

During the past eight years, science and technology took center stage both at the White House and in the public forum. Stem education was a cornerstone of Barack Obama's administration, and he championed Stem education throughout his presidency.

On Obama's watch, the US was on track to train 100,000 new Stem teachers by 2021. American universities began graduating 100,000 engineers every year for the first time in the nation's history. High schools in 31 states introduced computer science classes as required courses.

Like many of his cabinet choices, President-elect Trump's appointment of Betsy DeVos as secretary of education is darkly portentous. One of the country's most vocal charter school cheerleaders, DeVos has little experience with public education beyond demonizing it as the product of governmental overreach.

DeVos and her husband Dick have spent millions of their vast personal fortune fighting against regulations to make charter schools more accountable, campaigned tirelessly to expand charter school voucher programs, and sought to strip teachers' unions of their collective bargaining rights—including teachers' right to strike. Despite these alarming shortcomings, Trump seems confident that a billionaire with little apparent interest in public education is the perfect choice for such a crucial role.

There is no doubt that this appointment will affect the opportunities of students keen to launch a career in Stem. Private schools such as Carnegie Mellon University, for example, may be able to offer state-of-the-art robotics laboratories to students, but the same cannot be said for community colleges and vocational schools that offer the kind of training programs that workers displaced by robots would be forced to rely upon.

In light of staggering student debt and an increasingly precarious job market, many young people are reconsidering their options. To most workers in their 40s and 50s, the idea of taking on tens of thousands of dollars of debt to attend a traditional four-year degree program at a private university is unthinkable.

Enter Silicon Valley: No Need for a Degree Any More?

Solving inequality in tech has been a particularly challenging PR exercise for Silicon Valley. A report published by the Equal Opportunities Employment Commission in May 2016 found that just 8% of tech sector jobs were held by Hispanics, 7.4% by African Americans and 36% by women.

However, those numbers have done little harm to perceptions of Silicon Valley in general. Propelled by our enthusiastic consumer adoption of mobile devices, startup culture has become the latest embodiment of America's Calvinistic work ethic. Graduates struggling to find jobs aren't unemployed; they're daring entrepreneurs and future captains of industry, boldly seizing their destinies by chasing bottomless venture capital financing.

"Hustle" has become the latest buzzword du jour, and it seems as though everybody is working on an app, trying to set up meetings with angel investors, or searching for a technical co-founder—including Daniel Hunter.

The son of two engineers, Daniel has been fascinated by robots his entire life. He spent much of his formative years building elaborate machines with Lego blocks, and later joined a robotics club near Sacramento, California. Before long, Daniel and his team-mates were pitting robots of their own design against those of other teams, and even won first prize in a regional robotics tournament.

Daniel is now preparing to complete his bachelor of science in robotics engineering at the University of California, Santa Cruz —one of a small but growing number of colleges across the US to offer a generalized undergraduate degree in robotics.

In addition to his studies in robotics, Daniel has also been improving his coding skills, in part to sate his intellectual curiosity, but also to further hone his competitive edge.

Daniel, who works at a startup that is currently developing an iOS app for sales professionals, is a firm believer in the new gold rush. He told me of his admiration for the work of libertarian journalist Henry Hazlitt, his ambitions to become a world-renowned roboticist and technologist ("I'm 21 now, so if by the time I'm 45— Elon Musk's age—I've established myself as a world-class mechatronics engineer, I'll consider myself pretty successful") and that he doesn't believe everyone should go to college.

"I ask myself pretty regularly if the degree is actually worth it," he says. "There's a lot of side projects I could work on that might provide more value to my future than some of the classes I take, so it's hard to justify."

Daniel also told me that his experiences defy conventional wisdom that earning a college degree is the only pathway to success in today's savagely competitive job market.

"I talk to as many employers and startup founders as I can, and I hear the same thing over and over: degrees mean less and less, experience is everything," Daniel says. "In the age of Udacity,

Udemy, MIT's OpenCourseWare, it's very possible to do a bunch of small personal projects, display that experience to an employer, and get hired."

This appetite for alternatives to traditional higher education has driven intense interest in private programming schools and self-styled coding "boot camps" in recent years.

Intensive coding schools may be popular, but they have attracted more than their share of criticism—not least for their typically high tuition fees, low academic rigor, and vague promises of highly paid, full-time jobs upon completion.

On top of this, one of the most common arguments leveled against coding boot camps is that they do little to address the chronic underrepresentation of minorities and the exclusion of those from economically disadvantaged backgrounds. "I think programming boot camps have been fairly criticized for the fact that there's a lot of tension around the idea of economic mobility," says Adam Enbar, a former venture capitalist and co-founder of Flatiron School, one of the most renowned private programming schools in New York City. "The reality is that most schools are fairly selective and very expensive, which means they tend not to be serving populations that really need a leg up economically; they're really more often people who graduated with a good degree and want to change careers."

Founded by Enbar and self-taught technologist Avi Flombaum in 2012, Flatiron School has implemented programs designed to make careers in technology more accessible to marginalized groups.

"For three years, we've been working with the city of New York on something called the New York City Web Development Fellowship, where we run programs exclusively focused on low-income and underrepresented students," Enbar says. "We've done courses exclusively for kids from households with no degrees. We've done courses exclusively for foreign-born immigrants and refugees … When we enroll students at Flatiron School, we actually specifically look for people from different backgrounds. We don't want four math majors sitting around a table together working on a project—we'd rather have a math major and a poet, a military veteran and a lawyer, because it's more interesting."

We Don't Need Any More Food Delivery Apps—We Need Engineers

Developing a new iOS app may be more interesting than navigating the comparatively dreary worlds of logistics infrastructure, manufacturing protocols, and supply chain efficiencies, but America doesn't need any more messaging or food delivery apps— it needs engineers. The question, according to Enbar, is not whether future engineers earn their degrees from traditional colleges or not, it's about what a technology job actually is and how we, as a nation, view scientific and technical work.

In much the same way, many also believe we must examine the role of technology in primary education if we are to address growing concerns about labor shortages. Initiatives such as Hour of Code, a nationwide program that aims to highlight the importance of programming in K-12 education, have proven remarkably popular with educators and students alike.

According to Enbar, such initiatives are just one way America needs to examine its attitude toward Stem and traditional education. "I think the question we should be asking is 'Why is this important?'" Enbar says. "We have to ask ourselves why we're not mandating accounting or nursing or plenty of other jobs. The answer is that we're not trying to create a nation of software engineers—it's that this is becoming a fundamental skill that is necessary for any job you want to do in the future."

Despite these grave threats, when I asked Daniel where he sees himself in five years, he remained cautiously optimistic.

"I'll have my undergraduate degree and be several years into working," Daniel says. "I don't think I'll go to grad school. I'm not sure if I'll be working at a company or for myself—that largely depends on the opportunities I find once I graduate, and it's pretty difficult to predict that."

It is indeed difficult to predict how the gradual automation of the American workforce will take shape under Trump's presidency. One certainty, however, is that the interests of those Americans at greatest risk of professional obsolescence will continue to be sacrificed in favor of serving, protecting and benefiting wealthy, white conservatives—a trend we are likely to see across virtually every aspect of life in Trump's America and yet another betrayal of the predominantly working-class voters who believed Trump's empty promises on the campaign trail.

As Enbar observed, the most urgent question we must answer is not one of robots' role in the workforce of 21st-century America, but rather one of inclusion—and whether turning our backs on those who need our help the most is acceptable to us as a nation.

If history is any precedent, we already know the answer.

> *"The premise that automation will make human work superfluous flies in the face of all historical evidence."*

The Automation Argument Misunderstands Our Capitalist Economy

Katharina Nieswandt

In the following viewpoint, Katharina Nieswandt argues that increased productivity does not lead to a lighter work week or increased pay for the individuals on the front lines of the change. In fact, in recent decades, productivity has soared while work hours and wages have stagnated or declined. Nieswandt explains that this is a straightforward result of our capitalist society and that "technological progress results in more products, not in more leisure." Nieswandt is an assistant professor of philosophy at Concordia University.

As you read, consider the following questions:

1. What is the Automation Argument?
2. How does the author feel about the Automation Argument?
3. In a capitalist society, how do work hours and production relate to one another?

Philosophers, economists and other academics have long discussed the idea of "basic income"—an unconditional monthly check from the government to every citizen, in an amount at least high enough to cover all basic necessities. Recently, this idea has gained some political traction, even among conservative parties—but early tests in both Finland and Canada are shutting down, with officials saying they're too expensive.

One reason this idea has caught politicians' attention is the fear that large-scale automation will soon put many people out of work permanently, even as economic growth continues. (Truck and taxi drivers are currently the most discussed example.) Basic income is seen as a solution to the social problems that the predicted "technological unemployment" will bring.

In the past, the argument goes, there was a lot of work to be done. Hence income had to be earned by working, and government checks had to be reserved strictly for those who were unable to work. Income was deserved, a compensation for the burden of work.

But with less and less work to do, this system comes to resemble a twisted game of musical chairs: In the future, it will be mathematically impossible for everyone who wants a job to find one. We can therefore no longer deny income to those who don't work.

This might be called the "Automation Argument" for basic income. The Automation Argument is extremely popular; countless contemporary newspaper and blog articles take it as a premise. But the Automation Argument is false, and it impedes meaningful economic change.

A False and Dangerous Argument

Under capitalism, technological progress results in more products, not in more leisure. Factories that improve their efficiency don't shut down and send workers home early—workers keep the same hours and crank out more goods.

True, technological progress can cause temporary unemployment. But a look at history will tell you that, unless we switch to another economic system, there is no reason to fear (or hope) that automation will put people out of work permanently. (Contrary to recent claims, artificial intelligence will not change that point.) The Automation Argument simply misunderstands how our economy works.

Neither does the Automation Argument advocate fundamental economic reforms. It justifies basic income by the need to cushion the effects of automation, and that is the same reason we give for today's conditional welfare payments: The checks are a charity toward those who cannot work. So even if automation did cause widespread and permanent unemployment, a basic income for those affected would not be progressive or emancipatory.

Robots Have Never Reduced Human Work-Hours

The premise that automation will make human work superfluous flies in the face of all historical evidence. (Economists refer to it as the "Luddite Fallacy.") The dream that machines will some day do most work for us is almost as old as mankind. Since the early 20th century, that dream has seemed within reach, and predictions of the end of work abound.

In 1930, British economist John Maynard Keynes famously predicted that, within 100 years, only 15 hours of work per week would be needed to satisfy one's "absolute needs." In 1980, French philosopher André Gorz suggested a policy that would have increased free time for workers at the pace at which computers were then expected to increase workers' productivity: from a 40-hour work-week to a 35-hour week over the first four years, to 30.5 hours at the end of year eight, and so on.

And yet today, despite all technical progress, we still have to eat our bread in the sweat of our face. How is that possible?

It's the Economy, Naturally

The fact that automation never increased leisure time is an inherent consequence of our economic system. Whenever machines let us do something faster, we tend to just plow that extra time into making more, instead of taking that time off.

Imagine a worker in a shoe factory, who produces 100 pairs of shoes in an eight-hour workday. Now suppose that the machine she operates during these eight hours is exchanged for a new model which suddenly cuts production time in half: Our worker now produces 100 pairs of shoes in only four hours. In principle, the factory could keep shoe production constant, in which case the worker would have the rest of her day off.

That is a political choice a society can make. As of yet, however, we have always chosen the opposite: Capitalist societies keep work-hours constant and increase production. Our exemplary worker continues to work an eight-hour day, but is now expected to produce 200 pairs of shoes during that day (and usually at the same wage). As the tele-teacher in Douglas Adams' "Hitchhiker's Guide to the Galaxy" aptly explains: Until we reach the "Shoe Event Horizon," we will simply produce ever more shoes.

On the way there, technological progress will indeed wipe out some jobs, but new ones will arise in their places.

Productivity Climbs as Work-Hours Stagnate

Take the example of the U.S.: Work productivity—that is, the value produced per work-hour—has quintupled since 1947. On average, every hour that Americans work today yields five times as many (or as valuable) products as an hour worked by their grandparents. At the same time, however, work-hours per person did not decline.

Other industrialized countries have seen similar increases of work productivity without a decline in work-hours. Many European countries recently raised the retirement age, effectively increasing the absolute number of work-hours per life.

Certainly, the past is not always a guide to the future. Some argue that this time it's different because we will soon have artificial intelligence, so robots could take over even high-skill jobs. But it is unclear why that should make a principle difference if we keep our economic system: The principle of production increase over leisure increase applies independently of the type of job in question.

On top of that, the current changes seem rather small in historical perspective. Google or Airbnb might have introduced important new technologies or business concepts, but we are far from the often-predicted new industrial revolution. (And don't forget that the good old Industrial Revolution created more professions than it destroyed—in the high- and low-skill sectors alike.)

Like all new technologies, automated production does not, by itself, improve people's lives. If we want automation to result in more leisure for the average employee, then we need to make serious changes to our mode of production. (Yes, that is a political choice we have.)

Basic Income Would Not Change Much

There is a further reason to be critical of the Automation Argument for basic income. At first sight, this argument sounds revolutionary because we no longer need to do anything to deserve income. Let's face it, the argument says, technological development forces us to overhaul some moral beliefs near and dear to us, such as: "If any will not work, neither let him eat." These beliefs might have been reasonable for most of human existence, the Automation Argument concedes. But in a situation where we lack enough tasks to be carried out, it becomes cynical to consider people who don't work free riders.

The Automation Argument hence presupposes that we currently should work eight-hour days, and it presupposes that (at least by and large) each of us currently receives as compensation what we deserve, given our individual contribution.

In reality, incomes mostly reflect social hierarchies—as do beliefs about who deserves income. To see this, just consider the following three features of our income structure and what we think about them:

1. People who live off government transfers like welfare checks even though they could work are widely regarded as free riders. These people live off our work, and if that's not exploitation, then what is? There is no similar public grudge against people who live off our work by other means: by living off dividends and of government transfers like tax exemptions. While welfare recipients form the bottom of our social hierarchy, the idle rich are even admired.

2. Work is widely considered a burden, and income is seen as its deserved compensation. In reality, however, there is no correlation between how burdensome and how well-compensated a job is—otherwise, construction workers, cleaners and prostitutes would top the pay scale.

3. An increase in productivity legally belongs to the owner of the new technology, and few of us seem to mind that. In the example of the shoe factory, production doubled. The worker neither got more time off as a result, nor higher pay: The factory owner got more shoes to sell.

Is Income Today Deserved?

The Automation Argument does not challenge any of these three beliefs:

1. The income it advocates is unconditional, but it is justified in the same way as today's conditional welfare checks: It is a charity toward those who cannot work and have no capital.

2. Everybody else will continue to work and be paid in the same way that they are today. Those of us who still have a job will collect basic income in addition to our current

salaries (a gain partly annulled by the taxes paid to fund basic income). But there will be no fundamental reform of the economy.

3. Those of us who are laid off are not entitled to any of the gains that the new technology produces. The owner of the new technology alone is entitled to its proceeds, while all of our fellow citizens are now responsible to pay for our living (through taxes that fund basic income).

The call for basic income in order to soften the effects of automation is hence not a call for greater economic justice. Our economy stays as it is; we simply extend the circle of those who are entitled to receive public benefits. If we want economic justice, then our starting point needs to be more radical: We need to reconsider our deeply ingrained belief that wages and proceeds today are (usually) deserved.

"The average worker's salary peaked in 1973 and has declined over subsequent decades (while adjusting for inflation)."

Productivity Has Risen but Wages Have Not

Randeep Sudan and Darshan Yadunath

In the following viewpoint, Randeep Sudan and Darshan Yadunath argue that salaries have not seen increases at the same rates as productivity has increased. Regardless of whether the future is actually jobless due to advances in technology, the authors note that changes are certainly afoot as the age of disruptive technological innovation continues. Sudan is a former adviser of digital strategy and government analytics and practice manager for information and communication technologies at the World Bank. Yadunath has graduate degrees in economics and public policy and is a doctoral candidate at the University of Houston's department of economics.

"Are We Heading Towards a Jobless Future?" by Randeep Sudan and Darshan Yadunath, The World Bank Group, August 12, 2015. Reprinted by permission.

As you read, consider the following questions:

1. What have been some results of advances in natural language processing?
2. The automation of what type of machine is likely, according to one report, to lead to the elimination of 10 million jobs over the next decade to 15 years?
3. Explain the line of thinking of experts who say that new jobs are being created due to technological advances.

From the wheel to the steam engine, from the car to "New Horizons"—an inter-planetary space probe capable of transmitting high-resolution images of Pluto and its moons—from the abacus to exascale super-computers, we have come a long way in our tryst with technology. Innovations are driving rapid changes in technology today and we are living in a world of perpetual technological change.

In 1965, Gordon Moore—co-founder of Intel Corporation—hypothesized that the number of transistors on an integrated circuit will double every 18 to 24 months. This came to be known as Moore's Law, the ramifications of which are hard to ignore in almost any aspect of our everyday lives. Information has become more accessible to people at lower costs. Today's work force is globalized and there are few domains that are still untouched by technology.

Yet the very ubiquitous and rapidly evolving nature of information and communication technologies (ICTs) gives rise to fears of displacing more workers and potentially widening the economic gap between the rich and poor. Technological evolution and artificial intelligence are fast redefining the conventional structure of our society.

Jobs and Automation

Areas where computers are taking over conventional jobs include, for example radiology, a field of medicine that requires several years of extensive study to master. Systems such as the ones made by BD FocalPoint can interpret medical images and look for abnormalities such as tumors with greater speed and accuracy than humans can.

Advances in natural language processing have led to the creation of intelligent Interactive Voice Response Systems that are replacing traditional call centers and manual agents, resulting in higher efficiency and lower costs of operation for corporations. IPSoft claims that its cognitive agent Amelia can work along with human call center agents, and is able to learn and understand like a human.

Manufacturing companies in China such as Foxconn have plans to replace 1.2 million workers with robots to stay competitive. Rising labor wages in countries like Vietnam and Indonesia are hurting profits of companies such as Nike, who are already looking at alternatives to substitute labor with capital.

The rise of autonomous cars is likely to have huge impacts on jobs and employment. A study puts the total estimate of job losses due to vehicle automation at 10 million jobs in the next 10-15 years. The repercussions of moving to driverless cars can have a domino effect on a range of ancillary industries such as the automobile insurance market, automotive finance market, parking industry, and the automotive aftermarket with a suppressed demand for these services.

While jobs are being lost to automation, proponents of a counter viewpoint believe that several new jobs are being created due to technological advances. Their belief is that productivity and cost gains realized through automation make their way back into the economy helping citizens realize services at lower costs, which in turn leads to an increase in consumer savings and consumer spending resulting in more opportunities for employment in the consumer goods market.

Technology and innovations have increased prosperity in several developing countries. The Philippines and India have become major global outsourcing hubs employing hundreds of thousands of people. Mobile payment systems such as M-PESA in Kenya have revolutionized banking for the common man, while messaging systems such as Reuters Market Light have improved agriculture productivity in India by providing farmers with market prices, weather and crop information.

Rising Inequality in Wages Due to Automation

Technology has contributed to rising productivity. The post-world war era heralded accelerated employment, increased salaries of workers and raised prosperity levels.

However, since the 1970s, a strange phenomenon has gripped the American labor market.

The average worker's salary peaked in 1973 and has declined over subsequent decades (while adjusting for inflation). While labor productivity and salaries of ordinary private sector workers show a seemingly perfect correlation between 1948 and 1973, they move farther away from each other with every passing year after 1973 pointing to wealth accruing in the hands of business owners and investors as opposed to the average industry worker. Additionally, the share of US national income going to labor has plummeted since the 1970s.

Of the several theories that have been put forth to explain the above phenomena, the compelling role played by information technology and automation certainly cannot be ignored. In his book "Rise of the Robots: Technology and the Threat of a Jobless Future," Martin Ford states that the advent of Information Technology has replaced workers instead of making them more valuable, leading to increasing income inequalities between workers who possess the skills to adapt to tectonic technological shifts and those who do not.

Robots have largely been seen as machines that can perform routine, repetitive, non-cognitive actions. However, machines are already replicating human capabilities.

A combination of artificial intelligence (AI), dexterity and three-dimensional machine vision (the origins of which may be traced back to the Nintendo Wii video game console), give robots manufactured by Industrial Perception, a Palo Alto based company (acquired by Google), the ability to recognize, move and arrange boxes in complex sequences—a human skill that had not previously been emulated. In 2012, Amazon acquired Kiva systems, a warehouse robotics company that produces autonomous robots to move materials in large warehouses. Amazon has also been testing drones for delivering shipments.

Whether we will face the threat of a jobless future or not, the future of jobs and skills undoubtedly faces new challenges in the age of disruptive technological innovation. These trend-lines call for urgent action by governments to match jobs with skills to ensure shared economic prosperity and equal opportunity for all.

Automation of Labor

Periodical and Internet Sources Bibliography

The following articles have been selected to supplement the diverse views presented in this chapter.

Nellie Bowles, "Our Tech Future: The rich own the robots while the poor have 'job mortgages,'" Guardian.com, March 12, 2016. theguardian.com/culture/2016/mar/12/robots-taking-jobs -future-technology-jerry-kaplan-sxsw.

Utpal Chakraborty, "Impact of Modern Automation on Employment," BecomingHuman.ai, January 7, 2018. becominghuman.ai /impact-of-modern-automation-on-employment-by-utpal -chakraborty-e384a5cfebc3.

Kim Hart, "Tech Companies Pledge to Use Artificial Intelligence Responsibly," Axios.com, October 24, 2017. axios.com/tech -companies-pledge-to-use-artificial-intelligence-responsibly -1513306395-cd8dc8ee-be10-4bb5-a2cf-84030f495c7d.html.

Loukas Karabarbounis and Brent Neiman, "The Global Decline of the Labor Share," University of Chicago, 2014. faculty.chicagobooth.edu/loukas.karabarbounis/research/labor_ share.pdf.

Joshua Kim, "Robot Bartenders and the Future of Work," InsideHigherEd.com, July 22, 2018. InsideHigherEd.com/blogs /technology-and-learning/robot-bartenders-and-future-work.

Bernard Marr, "The 4th Industrial Revolution and a Jobless Future—A Good Thing?," Forbes.com, March 3, 2017. forbes.com/sites /bernardmarr/2017/03/03/the-4th-industrial-revolution-and-a -jobless-future-a-good-thing/#7bea35e944a5.

Steven Melendez, "Amazon and Walmart Add More Robots but Insist They Won't Terminate Jobs," FastCompany.com, December 15, 2018. fastcompany.com/90279838/amazon-and-walmart-add -more-robots-but-insist-they-wont-terminate-jobs.

Elizabeth Merritt, "Labor 3.0: New jobs, or a jobless future?," American Alliance of Museums, May 1, 2016. aam-us .org/2016/05/01/labor-3-0-new-jobs-or-a-jobless-future.

Tony Romm, "IBM Is Telling Congress Not to Fear the Rise of an AI 'Overlord,'" Recode, June 27, 2017. https://www.recode .net/2017/6/27/15875432/ibm-congress-ai-job-loss-overlord.

Ari Stein, "A Jobless Future Is Coming, Says China Tech Guru Kai-Fu Lee, and We Must Prepare Now," *Post Magazine,* October 18, 2018. scmp.com/magazines/post-magazine/long-reads/article/2166979/jobless-future-coming-says-china-tech-guru-kai-fu.

Jessica Stillman, "21 Future Jobs Robots Are Actually Creating," Inc.com, December, 6, 2017. inc.com/jessica-stillman/21-future-jobs-robots-are-actually-creating.html.

For Further Discussion

Chapter 1

1. Do you agree with Mark Paul that the automation of labor does not pose a threat to employment opportunities? Why or why not?
2. Compare David Trilling's argument that the future workforce will need to develop more creative skills and will need more education to Stephen Hawking's and James Bessen's positions. Which do you think is the best perspective?
3. Jessica Davis Pluess argues that an investment in technology and automation must include consideration of the impacts these advances will have on the current and future labor force. Which of her points is the strongest? Explain.

Chapter 2

1. Why does Moshe Y. Vardi argue that the future of automation is a force to be reckoned with and that mass unemployment will result from technological change? Are these points valid? Why or why not?
2. What is the strongest point behind Dominic Rushe's argument that automation is already part of the trucking industry and that it's only a matter of time before the industry is far more—if not fully—automated? Explain.
3. Larry Elliott argues that the latest wave of innovation poses a threat to today's "work"—and the appropriate pay that should come with it. Do you think this argument is valid? Why or why not?

Chapter 3

1. Erin Carson makes the point that automation is not necessarily the road to unemployment. What evidence does she provide to support this argument? Do you agree? Why or why not?
2. Sarah Marsh argues that teachers with a strong handle on technology will fare far better in the coming iterations of education. Do you agree with this position? Why or why not?
3. Bob Nilsson argues that personalized learning is a better approach than the traditional classroom setting. What points does he make to support this perspective, and do you agree? Explain.

Chapter 4

1. Aaron Smith argues that people are more concerned about being replaced by a person who will work for less than they are about being replaced by robots or their jobs becoming automated. What evidence does he provide to make these points? Do you think this is valid? Why or why not?
2. Dan Shewan maintains that robotic automation will have a profound impact on the workforce, reaching beyond the manufacturing tasks people have come to expect from robotic technology. What points does he make to support this and do you agree?
3. Randeep Sudan and Darshan Yadunath say that salaries have not seen increases at the same rates as productivity has increased. What examples does he point to in support of this idea? Do you agree? Explain.

Organizations to Contact

The editors have compiled the following list of organizations concerned with the issues debated in this book. The descriptions are derived from materials provided by the organizations. All have publications or information available for interested readers. The list was compiled on the date of publication of the present volume; the information provided here may change. Be aware that many organizations take several weeks or longer to respond to inquiries, so allow as much time as possible.

Future of Life Institute (FLI)

PO Box 454, Winchester, MA 01890

(800) 927-9800

email: max@futureoflife.org

website: futureoflife.org

The Future of Life Institute performs its work with the following mission in mind: "To catalyze and support research and initiatives for safeguarding life and developing optimistic visions of the future, including positive ways for humanity to steer its own course considering new technologies and challenges." FLI works to maximize the benefits of technology with limited risk, in areas including artificial intelligence, biotech, nuclear, and climate.

International Data Corporation (IDC)

5 Speen Street, Framingham, MA 01701

(508) 872-8200

email: press@idc.com

website: idc.com

Founded in 1964, International Data Corporation (IDC) is part of International Data Group. IDC is a global marketing firm that provides market intelligence, advisory services, and other related services to markets including information technology (IT), telecommunications, and consumer technology. The organization has over a thousand analysts and has done research in over 110 countries.

Leverhulme Centre for the Future of Intelligence (CFI)

Level 1, 16 Mill Lane, Cambridge, CB2 1SB, UK
website: lcfi.ac.uk

Funded by a £10 million grant from the Leverhulme Trust, this organization states that its vision is "to build a new interdisciplinary community of researchers with strong links to technologists and the policy world, and a clear practical goal—to work together to ensure that we humans make the best of the opportunities of artificial intelligence, as it develops over coming decades." Its projects cover issues involving and surrounding AI, including *AI: Futures and Responsibility, AI: Trust and Society, Kinds of Intelligence,* and more.

Machine Intelligence Research Institute (MIRI)

2030 Addison Street, Floor 7, Berkeley, CA 94704
(510) 859-4381
email: contact@intelligence.org
website: intelligence.org

Machine Intelligence Research Institute is a nonprofit research organization whose mission is "to develop formal tools for the clean design and analysis of general-purpose AI systems, with the intent of making such systems safer and more reliable when they are developed."

McKinsey & Company

55 East 52nd Street, 21st Floor, New York, NY 10022
(212) 415-1971
email: media_relations_inbox@mckinsey.com
website: mckinsey.com

Founded by University of Chicago professor James O. McKinsey in 1926, McKinsey & Company is a global management consulting firm with offices in more than 120 cities and 14,000 consultants worldwide. The company serves a range of private, public, and social sector institutions, and defines itself with the statement "We help our clients make change happen."

Robotics Industries Association (RIA)

900 Victors Way, Suite 140, Ann Arbor, MI 48108
(734) 994-6088
email: jburnstein@robotics.org (President)
website: robotics.org

The Robotics Industries Association is a North American trade organization founded in 1974. The organization provides relevant information to engineers, managers, and executives, and the website includes a range of resources, including job openings, events, expert perspectives, and news.

Robotics Institute at Carnegie Mellon University

5000 Forbes Avenue, Pittsburgh, PA 15213-3890
(412) 268-3818
email: robotics@ri.cmu.edu
website: ri.cmu.edu

The Robotics Institute at Carnegie Mellon University seeks "to combine the practical and the theoretical, the Robotics Institute has diversified its efforts and approaches to robotics science while retaining its original goal of realizing the potential of the robotics field." The organization's website includes a number of resources, including faculty contact information, research projects, video content, and details about a number of relevant publications.

US Department of Labor (DOL)

US Department of Labor, 200 Constitution Ave NW
Washington, DC 20210
(866) 487-2365
website: dol.gov

The US Department of Labor strives "to foster, promote, and develop the welfare of the wage earners, job seekers, and retirees of the United States; improve working conditions; advance opportunities for profitable employment; and assure work-related benefits and rights." The website includes career information and job openings as well as labor statistics, equal opportunity details, benefits information, and more.

US Equal Employment Opportunity Commission (EEOC)

131 M Street NE, Fourth Floor, Suite 4NWO2F
Washington, DC, 20507-0100
(800) 669-4000
email: info@eeoc.gov
website: eeoc.gov

The Equal Employment Opportunity Commission enforces federal laws that make it illegal to discriminate against a job applicant or an employee because of the person's race, color, religion, sex (including pregnancy, gender identity, and sexual orientation), national origin, age (40 or older), disability or genetic information. (It is also illegal to discriminate against a person because the person complained about discrimination, filed a charge of discrimination, or participated in an employment discrimination investigation or lawsuit.)

World Economic Forum

350 Madison Avenue, 11th Floor, New York, NY 10017
(212) 703-2300
email: forumusa@weforum.org
website: weforum.org

Established in 1971, the World Economic Forum "strives in all its efforts to demonstrate entrepreneurship in the global public interest while upholding the highest standards of governance. Moral and intellectual integrity is at the heart of everything it does." The World Forum believes that organizations should be held accountable to all aspects of society.

Bibliography of Books

Abbate, Dan. *Automation Manifesto: No Matter What Industry You Are in, You Must Automate Everything!* Scotts Valley, CA: CreateSpace Publishing, 2016.

Agrawal, Ajay, Joshua Gans, and Avi Goldfarb. *Prediction Machines: The Simple Economics of Artificial Intelligence.* Boston, MA: Harvard Business Review Press, 2018.

Armstrong, Stuart. *Smarter Than Us.* Berkeley, CA: Machine Intelligence Research Institute, 2014.

Avent, Ryan. *The Wealth of Humans: Work, Power, and Status in the Twenty-first Century.* New York, NY: St. Martin's Press, 2016.

Brynjolfsson, Erik, and Andrew McAfee. *The Second Machine Age: Work, Progress, and Prosperity in a Time of Brilliant Technologies.* New York, NY: W. W. Norton & Company, 2014.

Clark, Marcus. *The Future of Work: Human Value in a Digital World.* Pennsauken, NJ: Book Baby, 2015.

Danner, George E. *Executive's How-to Guide to Automation: Mastering AI and Algorithm-driven Business.* New York, NY: Palgrave Macmillan, 2018.

Eubanks, Virginia. *Automating Inequality: How High-Tech Tools Profile, Police, and Punish the Poor.* New York, NY: St. Martin's Press, 2018.

Farrell, Chris. *Purpose and a Paycheck.* New York, NY: HarperCollins Leadership, 2019.

Ford, Martin. *Rise of the Robots: Technology and the Threat of a Jobless Future.* New York, NY: Basic Books, 2015.

Gilchrist, Alasdair. *Industry 4.0: The Industrial Internet of Things.* New York, NY: Apress, 2016.

Gordon, Robert. *The Rise and Fall of American Growth.* Princeton, NJ: Princeton University Press, 2017.

Green, Neil. *Selected Topics in Automation.* New York, NY: Clanrye International, 2015.

Hyacinth, Brigette Tasha. *The Future of Leadership: Rise of Automation - Robotics and Artificial Intelligence.* Brigette Hyacinth, MBA Caribbean Organisation, 2017.

Murphy, Finn. *The Long Haul: A Trucker's Tales of Life on the Road.* New York, NY: W. W. Norton & Company, 2017.

Pugliano, John. *The Robots Are Coming: A Human's Survival Guide to Profiting in the Age of Automation.* Berkeley, CA: Ulysses Press, 2017.

Richards, Jay W. *The Human Advantage: The Future of American Work in an Age of Smart Machines.* New York, NY: Crown Forum, 2018.

Willcocks, Leslie P., and Mary C. Lacity. *Service Automation: Robots and the Future of Work.* Baltimore, MD: Steve Brookes Publishing, 2016.

Index